"What J. T. proposes for the loc it is mission critical. And it work how making space for deep discip to maturity. As the church heads i _____arism, she needs disciples who are deeply rooted, and it is her calling to make them so. For those compelled to move their churches beyond bare-minimum discipleship strategies, this book offers a way forward, drawing everyday disciples into the deeper things of God."

Jen Wilkin, author and Bible teacher

"The contents of this book are not theory or hopeful musings. They have worked. I had the privilege of serving with J. T. for five years as these convictions and concepts took root at The Village Church in Dallas, Texas. Hundreds and hundreds of laymen and women grew in a robust understanding of the God of the Bible, transforming their lives and the worship and fervency of our church."

Matt Chandler, lead pastor, The Village Church,
Flower Mound, Texas; president, Acts 29

"J. T. English combines razor-sharp theology with deep pastoral intuition to give us a book we badly need. It is amazing how much we can be doing in our churches without actually engaging in the sort of deep discipleship which will keep us all growing, serving, witnessing, and worshipping for the rest of our lives. J. T. shows us how the local church can become ground zero for theological passion and training. I look forward to applying his wisdom and hope many churches will do the same!"

Sam Allberry, speaker, Ravi Zacharias International
Ministries; associate pastor, Immanuel Church Nashville

"Pastor J. T. English is committed to helping us deepen our discipleship. There's just not much to the shallow Christianity that typifies too many of our churches, and too many of our lives. If you want to be both challenged and instructed on how you can change that, pick up this book. It might not take long to read, but its results may last a lifetime."

Mark Dever, pastor, Capitol Hill Baptist Church, Washington DC; president, 9Marks

"In *Deep Discipleship*, J. T. English smartly and accurately diagnoses what is perhaps the greatest challenge facing the American church: the tendency to call Christians to less engagement, not more. In a well written and easily readable book, J. T. lays out a biblical blueprint for how pastors, leaders, and laypeople can call the church to be everything it was meant to be."

Matt Carter, senior pastor, Sagemont Church, Houston, Texas

"When I reflect on *Deep Discipleship,* words that come to mind are these: biblical, needful, practical, readable. Grounded in the Word of God and fleshed out in the real life of the local church, my friend J. T. English provides a roadmap for developing and maintaining a faithful and healthy discipleship ministry in a local church of any size and location. My hope and prayer is that God will use this book to multiply disciples and disciple makers around the world."

Daniel L. Akin, president, Southeastern Baptist Theological Seminary

"This book is a rare combination of theology and practice on one of the most important aspects of the faith. Discipleship, according to J. T. English, is rooted in Scripture, situated in the local church, and aimed at mission to the glory of God. I hope *Deep Discipleship* is read widely, and I am confident that it will lead to the making and maturing of deep and holistic disciples."

Jeremy Treat (PhD, Wheaton College), pastor for Preaching and Vision at Reality LA; author of *Seek First* and *The Crucified King*

DEEP
DISCIPLESHIP

J. T. ENGLISH

DEEP DISCIPLESHIP

HOW THE CHURCH CAN MAKE
WHOLE DISCIPLES OF JESUS

B&H
PUBLISHING®
BRENTWOOD, TENNESSEE

Published by B&H Publishing Group
Brentwood, Tennessee

Dewey Decimal Classification: 248.84
Subject Heading: DISCIPLESHIP / CHRISTIAN LIFE /
DISCIPLESHIP TRAINING

Unless otherwise noted, all Scripture is taken from the
English Standard Version. ESV® Text Edition: 2016.
Copyright © 2001 by Crossway Bibles, a publishing
ministry of Good News Publishers.

Cover design by Darren Welch.
Author photo by The Southern Baptist Theological Seminary.

1 2 3 4 5 6 7 • 28 27 26 25 24

Contents

Diagnosing the Discipleship Disease

On Memorial Day weekend 2018 my wife and I were driving to see an orthopedic surgeon in Dallas. For several weeks she had been experiencing increasing amounts of pain in her right thigh. She is an active person, so we chalked it up to overuse—maybe she pulled something, or perhaps it was a slight tear. After weeks of stretching, icing, and lots of other remedies, we could not get the pain under control. We had to go see a doctor.

After asking us a list of questions, the doctors decided to perform an MRI to see if they could detect exactly what was going on. After the MRI we both sat nervously in the waiting room. All kinds of crazy things go through your head in a waiting room. Questions like: *Is this worse than we think it is? Is this not as bad as we think it is? Is everything going to be okay? Is this going to require surgery and rehabilitation?*

After a long wait we were called back to a small room to wait some more. We sat there for another thirty minutes, thoughts racing through our minds. Nothing could have prepared us for what would happen next. The doctor walked in, and some of the first words out of his mouth were, "I have got to be honest with you; this does not look good."

It was like someone knocked all of the wind out of me. What does it mean that this does not look good? What is wrong? How bad is it? I did not know what we were about to hear, but I did know that I was not expecting it. He proceeded to tell us that it looked like Macy had a high-grade malignant sarcoma—*cancer*. Sarcomas are a cancerous tumor; "high-grade" meant it was fast-growing and had a high likelihood of spreading to other parts of her body. In a single visit to the doctor, we went from thinking she had a pulled muscle to thinking about what her life expectancy might be.

Since it was Memorial Day weekend, he told us he wanted to see us first thing on Tuesday morning to do a biopsy to confirm the initial diagnosis. That was the longest weekend of our lives. We had countless people over to our house to pray and ask for healing. We shed countless tears, sang worship songs, read Scripture, and wondered how this would impact our two little babies who were three years and nine months at the time. We begged God to perform a miracle.

We went to the pool on Memorial Day to try to forget all that was happening and because the weightlessness of the water helped relieve some of her pain. I will never forget that we took a picture of all four of us in the pool. We were all smiling; we looked like a young, vibrant family without a care in the world. But on the inside we were terrified.

On Tuesday morning we went to the hospital to have a biopsy performed on the tumor in order to confirm the diagnosis. The biopsy lasted several hours, and I sat in the waiting room with our family and several friends. Over the next few hours doctors kept coming out to deliver news to other families. It seemed like lots of them were getting good news right there in the waiting room. Then a nurse came out to me and asked me to meet the doctor in a private conference room. I began to panic. *A private conference room? Why could he not share the information with me in the waiting room? Is it worse than he thought? Is it not as bad he thought?* I made my way to the conference room where he met me a few minutes later. He told me that the pathology report appeared to confirm the initial diagnosis, though he was a bit more optimistic that the tumor might not be as high-grade as he originally thought. However, he also said there were some unusual readings in the report and that he would like to send it off for further analysis at Harvard.

He told me that the treatment plan was likely going to be several rounds of radiation, followed by surgery to remove the tumor, followed by a fairly aggressive form of chemotherapy. His office began setting up appointments for consultations with radiologists and chemotherapists, and he would serve as her surgeon. Before we left, he instructed us not to begin any of her radiation treatment until we heard back from the pathologist at Harvard, just in case he had anything to add or changes with the diagnosis.

I could not believe he wanted to wait that long. If my wife had an aggressive form of cancer in her leg, I wanted to start treating it immediately. If it had a chance of spreading to other parts of her body, how could we let it just stay in her leg while we were waiting for another consultation? He assured us that though he was relatively confident in his diagnosis, that it is always better to be 100-percent confident before beginning any treatment plan. He said that the risk of misdiagnosing her illness would lead to mistreating her illness, which could be catastrophic. In this case, misdiagnosis and mistreatment could be fatal. In other words, we needed to know exactly what we were dealing with before we came up with a specific game plan for treatment.

So, we just had to play the waiting game. Over the next ten days we began all of our consultations and setting up her radiation schedule. These were some of the longest and hardest days of our lives. Her pain was increasing, and no matter what form of pain medicine she took, we could not get it under control. I began thinking about the nightmare of what it would be like to raise our two kids by myself. We spent time driving all over the city doing more scans on her leg and full-body scans to see if the cancer had spread anywhere else. We were in the depths of despair.

Around 6:00 p.m. on June 13, we got a call from the doctor, but because Macy's phone was on silent, we missed it. We frantically listened to the voicemail, and he said to call him as soon as we could because he had an important update for us. We called back . . . busy signal.

We called again . . . busy signal.

Third time, and we finally got through.

He began to tell us that he just received a report from the Harvard pathologist that suggested Macy had been misdiagnosed—she did not have cancer. *What? Misdiagnosed? Everything we had been doing, all the sleepless nights, all the scans, prayers, everything we had lived for the past few weeks was for nothing?*

If it was not cancer, then what was it? Her pain was still overwhelming, and we knew for sure that she had a mass in her leg. "Well, if it is not cancer," I asked the doctor, "do you know what it is now? And how confident are you?" He proceeded to tell us that he believed that Macy had a rare blood pool that formed as the result of some localized trauma, like tweaking a muscle, bumping her hip, or something like that. The small blood pool was beginning to form into a hard mass in her thigh, kind of like a bone. This condition is known as myositis ossificans, which is a benign tumor known to mimic more aggressive pathological tumors like a sarcoma. He said it was still going to be a long and painful recovery, but that it was not deadly or threatening in any way.

She had been misdiagnosed. She did not have cancer. This meant no radiation, no surgery, and no chemotherapy.

For the first few hours we just celebrated, cried, worshipped, called family and friends with the good news, and hugged each other. Eventually we began to process everything that had transpired over the previous few weeks. It was so hard to get our minds around the fact that she did not have cancer.

Those three weeks indelibly shaped the rest of our lives. We will never be able to un-live them. We cannot un-cry those tears. We will not get back those sleepless nights, begging God to act. Those three weeks, the misdiagnosis, the sleepless nights, the prayer meetings, the friends and family who pleaded with God on our behalf—I can remember all of it like it was yesterday.

The Danger of a Misdiagnosis

One of the many lessons we learned in that season was the importance of getting a diagnosis right. What if we had proceeded quickly with radiation before we heard back from the specialist? What if we had begun treatment too soon, a treatment that would have done more harm than good? What if we were so convinced she had cancer that we proceeded with confidence into a treatment plan for a disease she did not have? Even though our first doctor got the initial diagnosis wrong, I am thankful that he had the sense to get another opinion before moving forward with treatment, because in this case misdiagnosis and mistreatment could have been deadly. Getting the treatment right depends entirely on getting the diagnosis right.

I believe, similarly, that the local church has a discipleship disease. And without the proper diagnosis and treatment plan, we will do more harm than good.

Over the past several decades the Western church has noticed alarming symptoms of our discipleship disease. Some of these symptoms include people leaving the church; students dropping out of church after high school; attendance dropping; and perhaps most important, a lack of seriousness among our people about what it really means to be a follower of Christ. From an examination of these symptoms, we've come to think our disease is that the church has become increasingly irrelevant and requires too much from people who want to get involved. We see that we are losing market share in the world of ideas and in the rhythms of people's everyday lives.

The church seems to think our disease is that we've gotten too deep.

In order to treat this disease, we have sought to develop ministry strategies that require less of people, not more, strategies that focus on keeping disciples in the church rather than growing disciples in the church, and that view the pastor more as a marketer than a minister. We are on our heels, and we just want the bleeding to stop, so we have lowered the bar, and we have settled for a lowest-common-denominator discipleship.

Unfortunately, I believe many of us have misdiagnosed the disease and are mistreating the church.

Our ministry disease is not that the evangelical church is too deep, but that it is far too shallow. The symptoms of people and students leaving the church, or the lack of maturing disciples, or decreased attendance are symptoms that should tell us not that we are too deep but that we are too trivial.

People are leaving not because we have given them too much but because we have given them far too little. They are leaving the church because we have not given them any reason to stay. We are treating the symptoms of the wrong disease. Deep discipleship is about giving people more Bible, not less; more theology, not less; more spiritual disciplines, not less; more gospel, not less; more Christ, not less.

People are leaving the church not because we have asked too much of them but because we have not asked enough of them. We are giving people a shallow and generic spirituality when we need to give them distinctive Christianity. We have tried to treat our discipleship disease by appealing to the lowest common denominator, oversimplifying discipleship, and taking the edges off what it means to follow Christ.

Put simply, we have settled for a shallow approach to discipleship, believing that breadth will lead to depth. We have adopted philosophies of ministry that focus on growing crowds instead of growing Christians. We have asked our pastors to be marketers, not ministers of the gospel. In the church we focus on keeping people, but if they want to grow, they have to go outside the church. We think about how to keep people rather than how to form people.

I believe it is time for the church to ask some serious questions about our shared disease and how we can begin to create depth that might lead to breadth. Perhaps the church should start thinking about what it means to go deeper with fewer instead of going wider with the many. What if our cultural moment is inviting the church to embody the depth and substance of the Christian faith, not a shallow spirituality that appeals to the masses?

Not only that, but what if we could think through a philosophy of ministry that helped people grow and mature into deep and holistic disciples? What if we could develop and implement a philosophy of ministry that helped us not only appeal to the lowest common denominator but created a dissatisfaction with people staying there? What if we asked better questions about our philosophy of ministry that eventually led to the growth and flourishing of mature and holistic disciples in the context of the local church?

My hope in this book is to introduce a paradigm that will help local churches implement a philosophy of ministry that will grow and mature deep and holistic disciples. My hope is that local churches would grow in their confidence that if we focus on growing disciples we will build the church, but if we focus on growing the church, we may neglect building disciples. The primary way I intend to do this is to reframe the philosophy of ministry by asking better questions. By asking better questions, I think we will also come up with better answers.

The first question in chapter 1 is, "Why does deep discipleship matter?" Specifically, we will consider the nature and character of God and explore how his inexhaustible beauty, glory, and riches matter for developing deep disciples. In this chapter I will make the case that our philosophy of ministry should not just be informed by what God does but, more important, who God is.

The second question will be covered in chapters 2 and 3. Instead of asking the question, "Where *can* we form holistic disciples?," I want us to ask the better question, "Where *should* we form holistic disciples?" This is ultimately the question of space: where should deep discipleship happen? In these chapters we will look at why the primary context for discipleship is in the local church. Discipleship outside the local church is exploding because discipleship inside the local church is neglected, but we will see that Jesus has commissioned the local church specifically to teach, form, and develop maturing followers of Christ.

Not only will we see that disciples are formed in the local church, but that local churches should think intentionally about what spaces they are using to form holistic disciples. Are disciples formed primarily in the gathering, in-home groups, or in educational environments? In this chapter I will make the case that the local church should consider how community-based approaches to ministry would benefit by the retrieval of a rich understanding and implementation of Christian education. The context of discipleship has massive implications for what kind of disciples they will be.

The third question we will reframe in chapter 4 is about scope. Instead of asking the question, "What do disciples *want?*," we need to ask the better question, "What do disciples *need?*" Too many of our ministry philosophies follow a consumeristic mind-set that tries to give disciples what they want instead of giving them what they need. In order to make growing and maturing followers of Christ, how should the church intentionally be training their people so they may be equipped to equip others?

The fourth question, addressed in chapter 5, has to do with how we can make maturing disciples of Christ. Instead of asking the question, "How do we *maintain* disciples in the local church?," I want to ask the better question, "How do we *grow* disciples in the local church?" The local church should not just focus on how we keep disciples but on how we grow them. Local churches need to think through how they can develop a philosophy of ministry that will do just that. Depth with God is the way of holistic discipleship.

The fifth question is about sending disciples. Instead of asking the question, "Where do *some* disciples go?," I want to ask the better question, "Where do *all* disciples go?" As holistic disciples are being shaped and formed in the context of the local church, we need to be intentional about sending them into their spheres of influence to make more disciples. Discipleship never terminates with a disciple; all disciples are called to go make more disciples.

The final question is about scalability, sustainability, and strategy. Instead of asking the question, "*Can* my church do this?," I want to ask the better question, "Why would my church *not* do this?" This final question gets to the heart of why deep discipleship in the local church is scalable, sustainable, and strategic.

But before we turn to the *what* of deep discipleship, we must be reminded about *why* deep discipleship matters.

Instead of asking: "Where *can* we make disciples?," we will ask, "Where *should* we make disciples?"

Instead of asking: "What do disciples *want*?," we will ask, "What do disciples *need*?"

Instead of asking: "How do we *maintain* disciples?," we will ask, "How do we *grow* disciples?"

Instead of asking: "Where do *some* disciples go?," we will ask, "Where do *all* disciples go?"

Instead of asking: "*Can* my church do this?," we will ask, "Why would we *not* do this?"

Main Ideas

1. The local church has a discipleship disease. Without the proper diagnosis and treatment plan, we will do more harm than good.

2. The church seems to think our disease is that we've gotten too deep. In order to treat this disease, we have sought to develop ministry strategies that require less of people, not more. We have lowered the bar and settled for a lowest-common-denominator discipleship.

3. People are leaving the church, not because we have asked too much of them but because we have not asked enough of them. We are giving people a shallow and generic spirituality when we need to give them distinctive Christianity.

Questions for Discussion

1. Do you agree that the church has a discipleship disease? Have you ever tried to articulate it?

2. How have you tried—whether consciously or unconsciously—to treat this discipleship disease? Has your church lowered the bar or raised the bar of discipleship?

3. Are you convinced that lowering the bar is a mistreatment of our discipleship disease? If not, what would it take to convince you at this point?

To-Do List

1. Define in one or two sentences the church's discipleship disease.

2. Describe, at a high level, what an appropriate treatment plan might be.

3. Begin to discuss and write down ideas about how that treatment plan could be contextualized in your local church.

CHAPTER 1

A God-Centered Vision for Discipleship

I took a short sabbatical during the winter of 2019. It was my first sabbatical in ministry, and I am so thankful for the time away that was afforded to my family and me. For a few days I spent some time at Lake Tahoe alone. I wanted to use this as a time of renewal, rest, and rejuvenation. I had been to Lake Tahoe once before, but on this trip in particular, when I was there by myself, I was struck by the majesty of God's creation.

Lake Tahoe is one of the most beautiful places I have ever been. The beautiful Sierra Nevada Mountains reach up to crisp, blue sky and cascade down into the depths of the lake. On my trip I learned that the lake itself is one of the deepest in the United States, at 1,645 feet, behind only Crater Lake in Oregon. That translates into about five and a half football fields. I am not sure why, but that statistic was just stunning to me. Lake Tahoe trails only the Great Lakes in total volume, making it one of the deepest and largest lakes in the United States. If you take a boat out to the middle of the lake, the fresh mountain water is so clear that it can feel a little bit like the lake is bottomless—it just keeps going and going and going. Whether you are standing on the shore or looking down into the seemingly endless clear-blue water from a boat, the lake seems never-ending, vast, and bottomless.

Standing on the shore, I was reminded of the prophet Habakkuk's words to God's people: "For the earth will be filled with the knowledge of the glory of the LORD as the waters cover the sea" (Hab. 2:14). He writes these words as God's people are questioning God's use of Assyria and Babylon to bring his judgment upon them. Their kingdom is in shambles, they are practicing idolatry and wickedness, and they are wondering: *What are God's purposes in the world? Can this really be it? Is exile going to be our final destiny? Where is all of this heading?* What is the goal—the *telos* of the world?

This is the prophet's answer: *One day the whole earth, every single part of it—the sky, the mountains, the rivers, the canyons, all creatures, and all peoples—will be filled with the knowledge of the glory of the Lord.* Not only will the knowledge of the glory of the Lord fill them, but it will fill them as the waters cover the sea. The bottomless, infinite, and boundless God will cover all of his creation. The infinite beauty of God's presence will cover everything.

This is a stunning picture of where world history is heading. In the middle of their darkest moment, a moment of judgment, the prophet reminds God's people that all of world history is heading toward the kingdom and the presence of God. This is the future of God's world—it is our future. Their greatest hope, endless enjoyment of the presence of God, would one day be a reality.

The *Why* behind the *What*

Before we get into ministry philosophies, programs, and best practices, we need to remind ourselves of the why behind the what—the glory of God. The main aim of this book, the call to deep discipleship in our churches, is for the sole purpose of pointing ourselves and those we lead toward the infinite beauty of the Triune God. Success in ministry is not found in building programs but in building disciples—disciples who love God with all of their heart, soul, strength, and mind (Luke 10:27). Christ is the goal, not better or more impressive ministries. He is what we want.

The prophet Habakkuk is pointing us toward a future day when God's infinite glory will cover everything. He is showing us that the knowledge of the glory of the Lord is the goal of deep discipleship. It is the goal, because this is the future to which all world history is pointing. But the knowledge of the glory of the Lord is also the fuel of deep discipleship. It is the fuel because his presence alone is going to get us there.

I am not just advocating for a specific ministry practice. I am saying that our greatest desire in ministry is the presence of God. Specifically, in the local church we are motivated by this vision of the beauty of God. His presence is what we want. Ministry does not satisfy; God does. We want him now, we want him in the future, and his presence with us is the only way we are going to get there. Our ministry aim is to ask God to bring us into his inexhaustible presence, bottomless beauty, and infinite glory. Fellowship with the Triune God is where we are going, and fellowship with the Triune God is how we are going to get there.

God's desire is that one day the knowledge of the glory of the Lord will cover every square inch of his creation. God is working to bring a knowledge of himself to all of creation, and his followers want in on that now. If we know, beyond a shadow of a doubt, that God's purpose is eventually to cover all of creation with his glorious presence, then our instinct should be to get in on that now. Whole disciples of Jesus say, "If you are bringing your presence to this world, start with me, and start now." That is the instinct of deep disciples. We don't want to wait for tomorrow for the knowledge of God's glory to transform us. Discipleship is for today, not just for the future. We need disciples and local churches who not only look forward with eager anticipation to a future in the presence of God but who also want to be covered with the knowledge of the glory of the Lord today—now. Even though it may not look like it at times, this is the path the world is on, and disciples are already on that journey.

In order for the church to grow and develop a vision of deep discipleship, we have to start with the why behind the what. If we begin this book by talking about the what—programs, curriculum, and a philosophy of ministry—before we talk about the why—God himself—then it will be a complete waste of time. Ministry that is not oriented to the presence of God is dead. The why behind the what of deep discipleship is God. Why does deep discipleship matter? Because God matters. Nothing is more beautiful, lovely, pure, and limitless than God alone. Herman Bavinck gets it exactly right when he says, "God, and God alone, is man's highest good."[1]

I believe the greatest opportunity for the contemporary church is to recapture a radically God-centered vision for discipleship. Deep discipleship is more about reveling in the transcendence of God than it is a ministry practice. The source of true discipleship is not better programs, better preaching, or better community. All of those, and more, are hugely important tools, but the source of discipleship is God himself. Thus,

---

1. Herman Bavinck, *The Wonderful Works of God* (Glenside, PA: Westminster Seminary Press, 2020), 1.

at the heart of everything we do is the desire to grow in our love and knowledge of God.

We are called to love God with all of our heart, soul, and mind (Matt. 22:37). The Great Commandment actually repeats "with all" over and over again to remind us that nothing is worthy of our whole self but God alone. Discipleship, then, is about a redirection of our loves to the One who is lovely. The next curriculum, the next conference, or the next community group will only help you grow deeper in your relationship with Christ insofar as it attempts to reorient your love toward the Triune God. The opportunity in front of you, your ministry, or your church, is to retrieve the Bible's vision for the beauty and the centrality of God in all things. The invitation to deep discipleship is the invitation no longer to live with the next fifty years in view, but the next fifty trillion, and to aim our whole selves, our churches, and our ministries toward the kingdom of God.

In John 17:3 Jesus prays for his disciples to have eternal life: "And this is eternal life," he says, "that they know you, the only true God, and Jesus Christ whom you have sent." Jesus is always teaching his disciples that all of life is centered on growing in our love and knowledge of God. John Calvin noted, "The final goal of the blessed life rests in the knowledge of God."[2] This is the vision Habakkuk gave us—that all of cre-

2. John Calvin, *Calvin: Institutes of the Christian Religion*, trans. Ford Lewis Battles, vol. 1 (Louisville, KY: Westminster John Knox, 2001), 51.

ation is moving toward an awareness of God in all things. If we give people better ministry programs but fail to give them a radically God-centered vision for their lives, then we have failed miserably. In other words, the primary pathway of discipleship is not a curriculum, and it can't be programmed. The primary pathway of discipleship is God himself. God is the goal of deep discipleship.

When thought of this way, discipleship is not just a program but a total reorientation to reality. We begin to see who God truly is, who we are, what God has done, is doing, and will do in the world. In being reoriented to reality, disciples begin to view everything through a God-centered lens.

The opportunity in front of the church is not primarily found in better programs, better preaching, or a better philosophy of ministry. All of these are important, and the church should strive to be excellent in these things, but without a radically God-centered vision of all things, it does not matter how good at ministry we are. We cannot forget this. Great ministry practice that is not fueled by a great God is the greatest tragedy. The opportunity in front of us is to reorient ourselves and our churches to a God-centered vision of all things. We won't make any genuine progress in ministry that is not fueled by the presence of God. God is working in the world to accomplish his purposes of bringing about the knowledge of his glory to his entire creation, and the church's role is to align herself with the purposes of God.

It is important to point out at the beginning of a book about discipleship that will hopefully be read by ministry leaders and growing disciples that it does not matter how good our ministry plans are if they are not reorienting people to set their eyes on the God of the Bible. Deep discipleship is not simply a result of following a specific philosophy of ministry. If it were, discipleship would be so much easier. If all we had to do was write a curriculum, create a program, or cast vision for new ministry initiatives, most of our churches and disciples would be much healthier because we've gotten pretty good at those things. Programs, studies, and ministry initiatives are great, but they are not the fuel, or even the goal, of deep discipleship. Sure, we may be able to use these things efficiently and effectively to make disciples, but the question is: *Disciples of what?* Without the proper goal and fuel of discipleship, churches may have the most impressive ministries in the world, and they may be able to churn out disciples, but these won't be disciples of Jesus.

There is no silver bullet or perfect ministry paradigm that creates deep disciples. We should pursue excellence in all of these areas. However, if our primary focus is our own ministries, not God, then we will never make deep disciples.

We can't measure discipleship by how many people are in small groups, or how many are in our classes, or how many Bible studies they have completed. True discipleship can only be measured by a disciple's ability to connect all of reality to the

Triune God. When we think about discipleship, we are thinking about our ability to be reoriented to God, and we begin to see that God initiates discipleship, that God is the source of discipleship, and that God is the goal of discipleship.

Two Challenges to Deep Discipleship

There are many challenges that our churches face as we try to align ourselves, our churches, and our philosophy of ministry toward a vision of deep discipleship—too many challenges to highlight here. But I would like to highlight two acute challenges I think are more common than some of the others. What makes these challenges unique is that they often do not look like challenges but, instead, look like real discipleship. In other words, if we are not aware of these two challenges, we could be leading people into danger without even knowing it. These two challenges can be summed up as discipleship that leads to autonomy or apathy. If our churches want to make deep disciples, then we must be aware of how serious these ideas are and how to help our people navigate through them.

Self-Centered Discipleship

One of the greatest challenges facing the church is discipleship that centers on the autonomous self. The West is in the middle of a cultural moment that centers all of reality on the autonomous self. People's interest in spirituality is not waning, but the kind of spirituality people are increasingly interested in is a spirituality that is focused on the self. Bavinck's claim that "God, and God alone, is man's highest good," could be contrasted by a contemporary cultural mantra: "Self, and being true to yourself alone, is your highest good." We have replaced the transcendence of God with the transcendence of self.

Though this problem is uniquely clear in our cultural moment, it is not a new problem. Ever since Genesis 3 humans have viewed the love and knowledge of self as our highest good, falsely believing that the self, not God, is a bottomless well of beauty. Salvation, according to self-centered discipleship, is not found in knowing God but in knowing self. We are being told everywhere that truly finding ourselves is the antidote to our stress, anxiety, and confusion, but biblical discipleship says knowledge of God is the only true antidote.

In this turn toward the self, the church has, perhaps both intentionally and unintentionally, tailored its discipleship strategies to accommodate, and even perpetuate, this cultural shift. In other words, it is not just the secularist promise that salvation is found in self-improvement, self-actualization, and self-growth, but this is slowly becoming the promise in the church as well. In his book *No Place for Truth: Or, Whatever Happened to Evangelical Theology?*, David Wells comments on the disappearance of a God-centered vision for discipleship and the appearance of self-centered discipleship when he says that we can see "the shift from God to the self as the central focus of faith."[3] He goes on to highlight how this theological shift has led to a serious confusion about who God is, what discipleship is, and what the church's role is.

In Matthew 16, Jesus confronts this view of discipleship as self-improvement. At the core of the chapter is the incredible scene at Caesarea Philippi when Jesus asks his disciples, "Who do people say that the Son of Man is?" (v. 13). In verse 14, Jesus' disciples respond by saying, "Some say John the Baptist, others say Elijah, and others Jeremiah or one of the prophets." Persisting, Jesus continues his question by asking them, "But who do you say that I am?" (v. 15). In his famous response, Simon Peter replies, "You are the Christ, the Son of the living God" (v. 16). Jesus responds to his disciples by saying, "Blessed are you, Simon Bar-Jonah! For flesh and blood has not revealed this to you, but my Father who is in heaven" (v. 17).

I have heard it preached dozens of times that the question, "But who do you say that I am?" is the most important question anyone will ever answer—and for good reason. The identity of Jesus stands at the center of the Christian faith, but I want to suggest there is an equally important question. Jesus is not only interested in his disciples knowing who he is; Peter

---

3. David F. Wells, *No Place for Truth: Or, Whatever Happened to Evangelical Theology?*, 1st ed. (Grand Rapids, MI: Eerdmans, 1994), 95.

gets that part right. They must also know what he came to do and what is going to be required for them to follow him.

Jesus' identity can never be separated from his work, and our identity can never be separated from our call to follow.

Immediately after this scene the text tells us that "Jesus began to show his disciples that he must go to Jerusalem and suffer many things from the elders and chief priests and scribes, and be killed, and on the third day be raised" (Matt. 16:21). Peter, the same Peter who just got the identity of Jesus right, responds by rebuking Jesus. You see, for Peter, true human flourishing and true life are found in self-actualization, preservation, and improvement. He has just rightly answered that Jesus is the King, which is really good news for Peter. He is going to reign and rule with King Jesus! But it is going to look nothing like what Peter thought. How could the Christ, the King who came to rule, die on a cross? After all, Peter got into this whole discipleship thing because he thought Jesus was going to rule on a throne, and if Jesus was going to rule on a throne, then that meant Peter was going to rule as well. This is discipleship as self-improvement.

Jesus envisions discipleship differently than Peter does. If Jesus dies on a cross, and if Peter must follow him there, then that is going to get in the way of Peter's self-actualization. This is not who Peter wants to be—following Jesus to a cross is not "being true to himself." He wants to rule with Jesus in the kingdom; what does a cross have to do with that?

Peter has a view of the self that is consistent not only with the secular narratives of our day but with the human narrative that begins in Genesis 3—the narrative that tells us we are to grasp for an identity apart from God. Jesus confronts this false narrative by telling Peter and the rest of the disciples, "If anyone would come after me, let him deny himself and take up his cross and follow me. For whoever would save his life will lose it, but whoever loses his life for my sake will find it" (Matt. 16:24–25).

According to Jesus, discipleship is not about self-actualization or self-preservation; it is about self-denial. You will know yourself the most when you are carrying your cross. All of our self-actualized visions of discipleship and our own little kingdoms need to crumble and be crucified if the kingdom of God is going to reign in our lives. True self-knowledge comes not through being true to yourself but through denying yourself.

When we make discipleship about self-actualization, not self-denial, we fail to embody the way of the cross that Jesus beckons his followers to imitate. Discipleship is not the pursuit of self that transforms our view of God; the pursuit of God transforms the self—our whole selves. Matthew 16 shows us that the person of Christ cannot be separated from the work of Christ. It also shows us that the way to follow the person of Christ is to carry the cross of self-denial, not the crown of self-improvement. "For what we proclaim is not ourselves, but Jesus Christ as Lord, with ourselves as your servants for Jesus' sake" (2 Cor. 4:5). Disciples are learning how to slowly take their eyes off of themselves as they become more and more transfixed on Christ.

So, what does it look like on the ground when we succumb to the lie that discipleship is about being true to yourself? This is when our churches and ministries begin to offer people what they want instead of what they need. This is when disciples have a greater, more exhaustive knowledge of their Enneagram number than the attributes of God. This is when disciples are more inclined to read generic spirituality books than the Gospels. This is when disciples don't have a firsthand knowledge of their sacred text, or basic Christian beliefs, but have exhaustive knowledge of politics, sports, or entertainment. It is when disciples are more shaped by the practices and habits of digital secularism than basic spiritual disciplines.

So, how do we untangle ourselves and our churches from the pervasiveness of self-centered discipleship? We all need to be reoriented to who God is and who we are. Our local churches need to completely orient themselves toward the character and nature of God. Self-denial only makes sense if we get God instead of ourselves.

One of the most quoted lines in the history of theology is from John Calvin's *Institutes of the Christian Religion.* At the beginning of this masterful work, he says, "Nearly all wisdom we possess, that is to say, true and sound wisdom, consists of two parts: the knowledge of God and of ourselves."[4] Discipleship is being reoriented to who God is and who we are. That God is the Creator, and we are his creation. That he is perfect, and we are both beautiful as image-bearers and broken as sinners. That he is the Redeemer, and we are in need of redemption. However, many people take this quote from Calvin and apply it in a way that he never intended. Over and over I hear people use this line as a means to justify discipleship as the means to self-improvement. Calvin is not trying to get us to turn our attention to ourselves but to God, so that we can see our desperate need of him.

I can still remember the first time I went shopping for a diamond engagement ring. I had absolutely no idea what I was doing. The jeweler made me feel like I needed to have a master's degree in jewelry to understand how to buy a diamond. As the jeweler was explaining cut, color, clarity, and carat, I began to look through their collection. I was shopping on the budget of a college senior, which means things were a little tight. The diamond I was looking at honestly did not seem very impressive—especially for the price tag that came with it. Then the jeweler took out of the case with tweezers, placed it against a black backdrop, and gave me a magnifying lens to look at the diamond. Suddenly, the beauty and perfections that were inherently true of the diamond became evident to me. What

---

4. Calvin, *Institutes of the Christian Religion*, 1:35.

I could not see with my natural eyes all of a sudden became gloriously evident.

In other words, Calvin is not saying there are two diamonds worth studying, knowing, and magnifying: God and self. He is saying there is one diamond—God, and God alone—worth magnifying, and one black backdrop—self. Our job is to magnify God, not self.

Deep disciples are growing in their awareness that they are not a second diamond to look at through the magnifying glass. Instead, we are the black backdrop that shows how beautiful the true diamond is. As humans, our instinct is to magnify how great we are, but as followers of Christ, we are learning to proclaim, "Oh, magnify the LORD with me, and let us exalt his name together!" (Ps. 34:3). Christianity is not a religion of self-improvement; it is a discipleship program of self-denial. The way of Jesus is an apprenticeship toward self-forgetfulness—a growing understanding that we are the creation and that God is the Creator.

Deep discipleship, more than a philosophy of ministry, is really about helping your church reenvision the good life. Our people are being sold all kinds of visions of the good life. They are being constantly formed through books, media, and podcasts into their image of the good life. The Christian faith says that the good life starts and ends with God. It starts and ends with the idea that nothing is better than God and that he has given himself to us in Christ and in the gospel. Our churches cannot settle for Christianized versions of cultural discipleship, self-actualization, or self-improvement when we can have God instead. At the center of deep discipleship is the refrain that we want more of God and less of ourselves. We ourselves, and those we lead, must agree with John the Baptist: "He must increase, but I must decrease" (John 3:30). This is what Jesus was trying to teach Peter at Caesarea Phillipi. Discipleship is not a path to autonomous self-improvement that leads to a throne; it is a path of self-denial that leads to a cross.

Spiritual Apathy

The second major challenge our churches will face is the kind of discipleship or ministry programming that caters to spiritual apathy. We cannot settle for a kind of discipleship that lets people settle into boredom with Jesus as long as they are not bored with the church. In the church we are more concerned with apostasy than we are with apathy, but both are deadly to a vibrant walk with Christ. If our excellence in ministry is keeping people's attention rather than the beauty of Jesus, then we have failed. Becoming bored with the true Christ is impossible.

One of the reasons our people have grown bored with Jesus is that many church leaders have as well. We have settled for a cultural Christianity that is anemic and will not sustain disciples of Jesus.

The message of cultural Christianity is that God is merely good to us. The message of biblical Christianity is that God is *good for us*. The message of cultural Christianity is that we should seek God's goods. The message of biblical Christianity is that we should *seek God's goodness*. The message of cultural Christianity is that we should seek God so that he might provide for us. The message of biblical Christianity is that *God is our provision*. The message of cultural Christianity is that we should seek God in order to get things. The message of biblical Christianity is that we should *seek God to get the highest thing— namely himself*.

Do you see the enormous difference between those two theologies? The message of cultural Christianity and deep, biblical, holistic discipleship are at odds and cannot be reconciled. One of my greatest fears as a pastor is the idea that people may be satisfied with church but bored with Jesus. It terrifies me that people may enjoy the sermon, participate in small group ministry, volunteer on one of our many teams, and be completely satisfied by their experience—yet be spiritually apathetic toward the person and work of Christ.

These two competing visions have real-life implications for the life of discipleship in the local church. Discipleship is fueled by our beliefs about who God is. The message of cultural Christianity and the message of biblical Christianity are deeply at odds, but unfortunately, the message of cultural Christianity is what is forming the majority of the people in our churches.

Something like this was happening in the Colossian church. They were, by all metrics, a relatively healthy church. Paul begins his letter by expressing his gratitude for them (Col. 1:3). He encourages them to continue to grow in spiritual fruit (vv. 9–12), and he reminds them of the basic truths of the gospel (vv. 13–14). But then he turns his attention to the person and work of Christ (vv. 15–23). He does this because the Colossian church was growing apathetic toward Christ. They were not apathetic about ministry or church, but they were growing more interested in those other spiritual things than in Jesus. Apathy toward Christ but not toward ministry is a dangerous place to be. In the Colossian church there were people who were growing in their interest in spiritual things like angels, demons, and spiritual powers. There was another group of people who were interested in visible dominions, politics, and rulers. These people were elevating these visible and invisible created realities to the level of Christ. That is why Paul reminds them of who Jesus is—the image of the invisible God—and what he has done—created all things, visible and invisible. This is exactly what Paul says to a church that is apathetic toward Christ but is still spiritually hungry:

> He is the image of the invisible God, the first-born of all creation. For by him all things were created, in heaven and on earth, visible and invisible, whether thrones or dominions or rulers or authorities—all things were created

through him and for him. And he is before
all things, and in him all things hold together.
And he is the head of the body, the church.
He is the beginning, the firstborn from the
dead, that in everything he might be preemi-
nent. (Col. 1:15–18)

Paul is trying to remind them that everything is about
Jesus. It is entirely possible for a church to have a healthy budget, dynamic worship, relevant preaching, contemporary leadership principles, and a thriving family ministry, and still be in
danger of failing in its primary mission of making disciples of
Christ. He is correcting their apathy toward Christ by reminding them of Christ's preeminence. He is gently reminding the
local church that if we are known for anything other than the
preeminence of Christ in all things, then we have failed. When
we grow apathetic, we will find spiritual substitutes for our
ministries, but Paul is saying that apathy is corrected when we
remind ourselves of the preeminence of Christ.

We are living in a cultural moment where apostasy from
Christ is a real threat. It's entirely possible, and maybe even
likely, that many people who once professed Christ will walk
away from him. Apostasy is a real danger to the church, but
apathy is equally dangerous. This produces a Christianity
that elevates visible and invisible realities above the life of
discipleship.

This looks like Jesus and politics, Jesus and business, Jesus and sports, Jesus and fitness, Jesus and finances, Jesus and spiritual warfare, Jesus and coffee, Jesus and community, Jesus and other forms of spirituality. Anytime we elevate created things—visible or invisible—we aren't elevating them to Christ; we are bringing Christ down to them. We are not giving him the honor and glory that is due to him alone.

A domesticated Jesus will never produce deep disciples; a domesticated Jesus is not worth following. The best medicine for a church that has grown apathetic is to introduce them to the awesomeness of Christ, which is exactly what Paul is trying to do for the Colossian church: "He is the image of the invisible God" (Col. 1:15). Never lose your awe of who Christ is, what he has done, what he is doing, and what he promises to do in the future. He is the image of the invisible God; he is the Creator of all things; he is the Alpha and the Omega; he sustains all things. He is the head of the church; he is the resurrection and the life; he is God Almighty.

Discipleship is learning about Christ's supremacy over all things. It is truly companionship with Jesus through all of life.[5] A scheme of the devil is to get people to renounce their faith in Christ, but another scheme of the devil is for people simply to grow bored with Christ. Satan will do anything he can to get

---

5. Kevin J. Vanhoozer, *Hearers and Doers: A Pastor's Guide to Making Disciples through Scripture and Doctrine* (Bellingham, WA: Lexham Press, 2019), 60.

you to take your eyes off Christ. He knows that you, or your church, do not have to renounce Jesus to cease to be useful in God's kingdom; you just have to grow bored with him.

Deep discipleship is radically committed to a God-centered, a Christ-centered, vision of all things. One of the greatest mistakes we will make as we seek to grow in our own walk with Christ, and as we seek to help others deepen their faith, is that we will try to give people more than Jesus. True discipleship is not more *than* Jesus, but more *of* Jesus. Ministry is only worth doing if Christ is the One who gets all the glory.

The invitation to deep discipleship in the local church is the invitation to enjoy the infinite God—to invite him to cover his church with the knowledge of his glory, as the waters cover the sea. J. I. Packer asks these important questions of discipleship: *What are we made for? What aim should we set ourselves in life?* To both he answers: to know God.[6] He is absolutely right, and if we believe that, we also need to ask this question: *How can we structure our churches and ministries to help people toward that end?*

If God is who he says he is, then nothing is more valuable than deep discipleship. Everyone is a disciple of something, but only the Triune God invites us into deep, holistic, never-ending fellowship. One of my greatest hopes in this book, far

---

6. J. I. Packer, *Knowing God,* 20th anniversary ed. (Downers Grove, IL: InterVarsity Press, 1993), 33.

beyond a philosophy of ministry, is that our churches will be reminded of who God is. He is more beautiful than we can ever imagine. Discipleship that is geared toward self-improvement or that caters to spiritual apathy evaporates when we see him for who he is.

If we do not adopt discipleship strategies in the local church with the sole intent of inviting people into the depths of beauty that can only be found in the Triune God, then our disease will only get worse. The heartbeat of deep discipleship is to see our churches, sermons, groups, studies, and kids ministries once again captivated by the beauty of the Triune God above all else. The foundation of deep discipleship is the glorious truth that God doesn't just give us ideas, plans, and ministry philosophies for churches; he gives us himself. God is the goal of deep discipleship, and God is the means of deep discipleship. He is where we are going, and he is how we will get there. Whether we are standing on the shore, just beginning our discipleship journey, or hoping to swim into the depths of Christian maturity, we know we want more. Not more *than* Jesus, but more *of* Jesus. We want more of him because he is not just good to us; most important, he is good for us.

Discipleship should be deep because God is inexhaustible. He invites his church into rich and deep fellowship because his goodness is indeed bottomless, and you can never exhaust the bottomless beauty of God. Along with Paul we proclaim, "Oh, the depth of the riches and wisdom and knowledge of God!

How unsearchable are his judgments and how inscrutable his ways!" (Rom. 11:33). The invitation to deep, holistic discipleship is first and foremost an invitation to see God for who he is, our highest good.

Main Ideas

1. God's desire is that one day the knowledge of the glory of the Lord will cover every square inch of his creation. That is the main aim of deep discipleship—to point ourselves and those we lead toward the knowledge of the infinite beauty of God.

2. Discipleship is not just a program but a total reorientation to reality. We begin to see who God truly is, who we are, and what God has done, is doing, and will do in the world.

3. There are two main challenges to deep discipleship: self-centered discipleship and spiritual apathy. In the former, salvation is not found in knowing God but in knowing and being true to self. In the latter, we settle for a kind of discipleship that lets people settle into boredom with Jesus as long as they are not bored with the church.

Questions for Discussion

1. How is a God-centered vision for discipleship different from other paradigms?

2. If you were to take an honest inventory of your church, would you say that your discipleship operates within a God-centered vision, or some other (man-centered, entertainment-centered, morality-centered, etc.) vision?

3. Have you faced either or both of the two main challenges to discipleship in your church? If so, how have you responded to them?

To-Do List

1. Read Habakkuk 2:14. Spend some time praying that your church would be "filled with the knowledge of the glory of the LORD as the waters cover the sea." Ask God to show you what must change in your church for this to be a reality.

2. Take stock of the different programs and ministries in your church. How many would you say are operating with a God-centered vision of discipleship?

3. Identify which main challenge to discipleship is a greater threat to your church. Pray for God's help against this challenge, and begin brainstorming some ways you can lovingly and graciously correct and redirect this posture.

CHAPTER 2

The Church: Where Whole Disciples Are Formed

Growing up, I didn't know the Lord. I was raised by wonderful parents in a safe and loving environment, but to my memory I never heard, or perhaps I just never understood, the gospel. I went to church from time to time, and at one point I was even confirmed in a church, but I certainly didn't understand the gospel or have a vibrant relationship with Christ. I remember having a Bible in my room when I was a kid, and sometimes I would read it; but like a lot of people, I would get confused somewhere in Leviticus or Numbers and put it down.

When I went to college, I was randomly placed with a roommate who I had never met before. After the first few weeks of school, he began inviting me to a campus-ministry

Bible study that was going to meet in the laundry room in the basement of the freshman dorm. Not only did I not want to spend my Tuesday nights of my freshman year of college studying the Bible with a bunch of other freshman guys, but it is hard to think of a stranger place to hold a Bible study than a laundry room of a dorm basement!

Every week, on Monday or Tuesday before the study, he would ask me, "Do you want to come to Bible study with me this week?" I was able to hold off his press for the first few weeks, but I soon realized that he was not going to stop asking until I went with him. Eventually I decided that I should go, just once, in hopes that he would not ask me anymore.

We walked down to the basement together, and I took a teen study Bible that I had from my confirmation. If I am honest, I was terrified. I was terrified that I was going to be seen as an impostor, or that I was going to be unwelcome, or that I would be asked a question I could not answer. The first few minutes we had a cordial conversation, then an awkward icebreaker exercise. When we eventually sat down, everyone around me began grabbing their Bibles. We were told to open up our Bibles to the book of Jonah.

Panic ensued.

I had never even *heard* of the book of Jonah; how in the world was I supposed to find it? Why could we not be in the book of Psalms or one of the Gospels? I knew how to find those, but Jonah? I quietly tried to thumb through the pages of my Bible, but unfortunately for me, Jonah is a small book, and I couldn't find it. More panic ensued. Did I have a Bible that did not include the book of Jonah? Did their Bibles have extra books of the Bible? Was this some kind of cult? I thought that maybe I could just look at the contents but decided against it because then they would know I was an impostor. Eventually the leader, a sophomore named Nate who was sitting right next to me, saw what was going on. Without making me feel awkward, or like an impostor, he used his own finger to open my Bible to the right page. My anxiety slowly began to subside.

I will never forget what happened next. I heard, for the first time I can remember, that God was gracious. He was gracious to a disobedient prophet who had defiantly disobeyed a direct command from God. How could this be true? In my mind the only appropriate response to disobedience was discipline and judgment. While I learned that those were part of the story as well, I was stunned by God's grace. Does God really extend grace to sinners? I mean, in the face of direct disobedience to God, Jonah could still receive grace and forgiveness and, on top of all of that, then be called on to proclaim God's grace to others? This message absolutely stunned me. I then began to wonder if grace like that was available to everyone—maybe someone like me.

The next day the sophomore who led the Bible study invited me to go to the student center for lunch to discuss what we learned the night before. He could tell that not only was I confused for most of it but that I was becoming more interested in what the rest of the Bible had to say. We ordered from Burger King and sat down in the student center at Colorado State University. As I was eating my hamburger, he pulled out a small booklet, that I now know is called the "Four Spiritual Laws." In the most uncompelling gospel presentation in the history of the world, he said, "I am supposed to read this with you." Seriously. No reason, no lead-in, nothing. Just, "I am supposed to read this with you."

I could tell he was nervous as he began to read. He said, "(1) God loves you and created you to know him personally." Without looking up, he flipped the page and continued, "(2) Man is sinful and separated from God, so we cannot know him personally or experience his love." He briefly looked up. I was going to ask him a question to try to break some of the tension, but before I could get a word out, he continued to read. "(3) Jesus Christ is God's only provision for man's sin. Through him alone we can know God personally and experience God's love." This point was the one I was most interested in talking to him about, so I figured he would stop there, but he continued, "(4) We must individually receive Jesus Christ as Savior and Lord; then we can know God personally and experience his love." At that moment I met Jesus for the first time. With a Whopper in my mouth, I said yes to Jesus Christ as my Lord and Savior.

If this story shows anything, it's that evangelistic methods don't save people; God does. I came to faith through the faithfulness of an awkward sophomore college student who was being obedient to disciple students through Scripture and to share the gospel.

I spent the next few years bouncing around between campus ministry and church, just trying to figure out what it meant to be a Christian. I was eating up anything and everything I could get my hands on related to discipleship. I desperately wanted to be formed, and I wanted to grow. I went on a few mission trips, learned how to share my faith through the campus ministry, and also met my future wife through the campus ministry. I could not get enough of this stuff. My future mother-in-law called me a "spiritual sponge."

One thing I began to notice was that a lot of my Christian friends, who had been walking with the Lord for years, seemed not to be all that interested in growing. Most of them were content with where they were in their faith and did not express a lot of interest in growing.

As we were wrapping up college, I was feeling like my growth was stunted. Just like my friends, I was having a hard time taking the next steps in my faith. By this point I had been a Christian for almost four years, and I felt like I was not where I wanted to be in terms of growth, development, and maturity. I wanted to know how to read and understand my Bible. I wanted to understand the basic beliefs of the faith. I wanted to know how to practice basic spiritual disciplines. I basically wanted to know how I could grow as a Christian, but I was realizing that I did not have a guide.

My discipleship felt aimless because my discipleship was churchless. Up until this point, most of my development and growth happened outside the church. I was hoping the church would be the place I could take the next steps toward learning the story of Scripture, the basics of the faith, and basic spiritual disciplines. Surely the local church was the place I could find these things.

"You Need to Go to Seminary"

We were having one of our premarital sessions with our pastor, whom I deeply respect. He asked us about our future plans for jobs, family, etc. Specifically, he asked, "What are you going to do after you graduate from college?" I responded by saying something like, "I am not sure, but I know that the most important thing to me right now is growing in my relationship with Christ."

Looking back on that conversation, I don't think I was expressing a call to ministry. I was simply expressing what I thought was a call into deeper discipleship, to taking steps of maturity as a Christian. I was trying to tell him that regardless of what my future vocation was, my highest priority was growing in my relationship with Christ. In hindsight, I was trying to say that I wanted to be a deep disciple. I was less interested in what I wanted to do and more interested in who I wanted to be.

My pastor looked a bit surprised and said, "Oh, you want to really grow? You need to go to seminary for that." "What is seminary?" I asked. I was so far outside of the Christian subculture that I had never even heard of seminary, but his answer, nonetheless, seemed strange to me. Why can't I grow and be trained to do these things in the church? Isn't the church supposed to disciple me? Isn't that what a pastor is supposed to do?

In retrospect, this conversation revealed one of the most tragic lies most American Christians believe today: that we have to leave the church in order to lead in the church.

Don't get me wrong—I ended up having an incredible experience in seminary. In fact, my years in seminary were the most formative years of my life. But at that time I did not understand that we had a system in which churches were relying on outside organizations to make deep disciples. Were all churches delegating growth and discipleship to other institutions and organizations? I didn't go to seminary to be an academic; I had to go to seminary to learn how to be a disciple. I will fight for the importance of seminaries because I strongly believe that they, and lots of other organizations, are invaluable as they help us train, equip, and send some of the finest men and women in the world into ministry. But this was different from that. It seemed like the church was not simply recommending seminary to supplement the discipleship of the church, but it was delegating its responsibility to make disciples.

Let's be clear: the church is called to make disciples, and it is time for us to stop delegating our responsibility. Other organizations can come alongside the church, but they can never replace the church.

A lot of discipleship—from beginning to end—happens outside the church. That is because we have asked the question, "Where *can* discipleship happen?," instead of asking the better question, "Where *should* discipleship happen?"

I was teaching at a conference several months ago in a room full of church leaders. I asked them to raise their hand if the majority of their formation happened outside the church. Over 80 percent raised their hand. Again, these are men and women who are committed to the ministry of the gospel and to the local church, yet most of their most significant formation happened outside the church. This is not just my story; it is the story of countless people who came to faith outside of the church and who were primarily discipled outside of the local church. We were saved through a Christian organization and tried to get involved in the church, but in order to be formed and shaped, we had to pursue outside opportunities for development. Bible colleges, seminaries, Bible studies, campus ministries, missions organizations, and other nonprofits have stepped in to fill the gap local churches have left. Praise God for these organizations, but they will never be able, nor do they want, to replace the local church.

This is why I am writing this book: I believe with every fiber of my being that the local church is God's primary means of making holistic disciples of Christ.

The local church is meant to be the primary spiritual guide for disciples who are on the journey of growing deeper in the love and knowledge of God. The local church is the place where we are formed, equipped, and sent out to make more disciples.

Think about your own discipleship journey. Where did most of the growth happen for you? Did it happen on the mission field, in a college or seminary, through an on-campus college ministry, or in the local church? I love hearing stories of rich, robust, and deep discipleship happening in our local churches, but in my experience they are too few and far between. God is definitely using his church to fulfill her mission, but if I am honest, most stories I hear tell of the most significant aspects of formation happening outside of the church.

If that is not your story, then praise God. But it is important to realize that is the story for a lot of us. What would it look like for us to really believe that God's mission is taking place primarily through the local church—your local church? Do you have the conviction and belief that the church is the primary context for holistic discipleship and, if so, do you have a philosophy and practice of discipleship to execute on that conviction?

Disciple Your Next Pastor

How much do you currently rely on outside organizations to make disciples? Do you use them to supplement discipleship, or are you delegating discipleship to them? Again, the church needs outside organizations for specialized training—that is not what I am talking about. I am simply talking about your desire, ability, and practice to help someone move from not believing to believing and then from immature to mature faith. Someone should be able to come to faith, grow in the faith, and walk in Christian maturity solely from being formed by a local church. That is the basic sequence of the gospel. We are orphans who have been adopted into Christ's family. Then, as adopted infants, we learn how to grow into mature members of the household—all of which can happen in and through the local church.

Here is an interesting case study I ask myself from time to time. Let's say that right now there is a nonbeliever named Jake at the local coffee shop close to your church. What would it take for your church to meet Jake, a nonbeliever, and provide opportunities and training for Jake to eventually become the next lead pastor in twenty years?

First, you would need to have a culture and practice of evangelism so that Jake would have the opportunity to hear the gospel, repent of his sins, be regenerated by the power of the Holy Spirit, and be welcomed into the church family. Then, you would need to have community-based discipleship

environments that train and equip him in the basics of the
faith. Perhaps classes on how to read the Bible, the basics of
the faith, spiritual disciplines, etc. These opportunities would
need to be sequenced in such a way as to have introductory
environments and advanced environments. In other words,
you would need to think about both accessibility and growing in maturity.

Do you think your church could disciple its next lead
pastor?

How about a young woman named Jill who comes to services occasionally but is not a believer? Could you develop her
into your next women's director or Bible study teacher? Do you
have an established pathway for her to hear and respond to the
gospel and get the right kind of training to grow into a mature
Christian? Would you have to delegate a lot of it to outside
organizations, or would you just use them as supplementary to
what is already going on in your church?

This is an exercise I think about regularly in my own ministry context. What if the next lead pastor of our church, or
our next women's director, is not yet a Christian—am I providing opportunities for them to hear the gospel, respond to the
gospel, be formed by the gospel, and learn to communicate
the gospel—all in the context of the local church? Of course, I
might want him to get specialized training outside the church
as well, but would I be able to build a foundation for him, or
would he be almost entirely reliant on outside organizations for

his growth and development? Put simply, can you form a pagan into a pastor?

This example does not just apply to trying to develop pastors or ministry leaders. This is equally applicable to anyone, in any vocation, in any age group. Is your church equipping business leaders to be faithful in their context? Are you helping moms and dads faithfully embody the gospel in their homes as they seek to disciple their children? Are you providing opportunities for your church to learn how to share their faith in their spheres of influence?

To put it bluntly, what if an eighteen-year-old new believer, just like I did with my pastor, came to you and said, "I want to grow as a disciple."? What would you tell him? Is your church prepared to receive an eighteen-year-old kid, like me, and slowly develop a maturing Christian over the next few decades?

What the Local Church Is

The local church is the primary place that God intends to make and form holistic disciples. We cannot disconnect the task of deep discipleship from the institution that owns it: the local church. The local church is the tool, God's providential instrument, that he uses to shape and form his people into maturing followers of Christ. The local church is where we are sanctified in Christ Jesus (1 Cor. 1:2), built up in the faith (1 Cor. 14:12). It is where the gospel is proclaimed (2 Cor. 8:18), where

Christ reigns as head (Col. 1:18). It is where holistic disciples are formed. The local church is not just one of many organizations God uses equally in his mission to make disciples; it is the primary context for holistic discipleship.

I believe that when discipleship happens in the context of the local church, it can and should be qualitatively different from discipleship that happens outside the local church. That conviction is formed not because of what the local church does but, more important, because of what the local church is.

Every local church shares in four distinctives that uniquely set it apart as the primary context for deep discipleship: place, people, purpose, and presence. Deep discipleship is grounded in a specific place (wherever it meets), with a specific people (the church family), for a specific purpose (mission and Christlikeness), and empowered by God himself (presence). This definition is also intentionally Trinitarian—the Father adopts his children into his universal and local family through the work of Christ the Son in order to equip them for mission and Christlikeness through the indwelling and empowering presence of the Holy Spirit. This has been God's mission since Pentecost, and that mission continues in Christ's church today, which makes the local church the ideal context for holistic discipleship.

Place

First, the local church is in a place. It is visible and situated. Historically, theologians have made an important distinction between the local church and the universal church. The universal church, according to Gregg Allison, "is the fellowship of all Christians that extends from the day of Pentecost until the second coming, incorporating both the deceased believers who are presently in heaven and the living believers from all over the world."[1] The universal church is made visible by the local church in embodied, temporal, and contextual congregations. The local church is manifested in local communities of people who regularly gather to worship the Triune God, proclaim his Word, participate in the ordinances/sacraments, carry out church discipline, and engage non-Christians with the gospel.

These local communities of faith are visible and situated. They are visible because they have locations, leaders, members, etc. They are situated because they are birthed in, and minister to, a specific context. Local churches are visible manifestations that testify to the gospel in specific contexts.

The universal church and the local church are both indispensable elements to God's purposes. Christians are meant to be encouraged, exhorted, and formed by both the universal and the local church. We are formed by the universal church

---

1. Gregg R. Allison, *Sojourners and Strangers: The Doctrine of the Church,* Foundations of Evangelical Theology (Wheaton, IL: Crossway, 2012), 20.

when we are taught and accept the faith that has once been delivered to the saints (Jude 3), when we learn from saints from centuries past, or when we listen to sermons, read blogs, or are shaped through worship music from other congregations. The universal church reminds us that we should read Irenaeus, Athanasius, Augustine, and others church fathers; we are meant to celebrate the work of the Reformers and learn from their insights; we should also engage in dialogue with brothers and sisters from other denominations, churches, and ministries. We are meant to bridge denominational lines, pray for one another, and encourage one another in the faith. Seminaries, Bible colleges, community Bible studies, Christian publishers and content creators, and campus ministries are beautiful manifestations of the universal church contributing to the health and vibrancy of the church as a whole. However, no matter how beneficial these expressions of the universal church may be, they can never replace the visible and situated local church. We should all participate in expressions of the universal church, but participation in the universal church must be grounded in participation in the local church.

The point I am making is this: where discipleship happens matters. Virtual discipleship cannot create deep disciples. Deep discipleship is intensely local. Formation is meant to be personal, embodied, and incarnational. A blog, an online professor, or a video-streamed sermon may be able to aid discipleship, but they cannot form disciples the way the local church can. We are in danger of adopting primary pathways of discipleship that are digital and disembodied. For example, with the rise of podcasts or online "churches," disciples can stream messages from any pastor or church they want. We have access to some of the best digital resources imaginable, but the digital and disembodied discipleship strategy will never form holistic disciples. Digital resources should certainly be used to supplement what the local church is doing but should never replace embodied discipleship. Pastors and ministers are called by God to shepherd the flock of God in front of them, not on their Twitter feed.

Holistic discipleship is meant to be visible and situated. Why? Because the Christian faith is inherently incarnational. In our digital and disembodied world, place matters more than ever. Holistic discipleship in the local church is possible when we emphasize that discipleship is in person, it is visible, it is messy, it is incarnational. The Christian faith is essentially fleshly—visible: "And the Word became flesh and dwelt among us, and we have seen his glory, glory as of the only Son from the Father, full of grace and truth" (John 1:14). In the incarnation God the Son demonstrates for us the importance of visibility and context. The Son condescends to his creation in order to make himself known. He did it in time, visibly, and contextually. In a time in which discipleship is trending toward the digital and the disembodied, the local church is the place where we are able to show that formation is not solely intellectual and immaterial but also physical. We are formed by our places, and we form our places. The local church shows that discipleship is not inherently gnostic or disembodied but deeply human and incarnational.

Why do place and context matter? Because our whole person matters to God. Discipleship is not just the transfer of ideas but the transformation of the whole person. It is not just the shaping of minds but also the shaping of persons. In the local church we have the opportunity to express that in beautiful ways.

Though this is not an example from the local church, it is an example of the importance of place in discipleship. When I was a seminary student, one of the faculty members, well known for his expertise in the New Testament, walked through a serious family tragedy. His wife, while riding her bike, had a serious accident and withstood significant injuries, specifically to her brain. There was a time when they were not sure what her mental capacities would be—if any. Watching that professor over the next few weeks was as formative as any other experience in seminary. He was not just a great professor because he taught excellent content. He was a great professor because he showed us how to trust God in the midst of deep suffering. I could never have learned this if I was taking his class online or simply reading his book. I learned to trust his teaching because I was learning to trust his life. His life was the curriculum that semester, not the syllabus.

That is why embodiment is indispensable to forming whole disciples. We are meant to share not just great ideas but also our lives with one another. We can only share our lives together if we commit ourselves to embodiment and relationship that is visible and situated. Local churches have an opportunity to call people to this kind of discipleship in a unique way.

People

We have discussed the importance of place for discipleship—that discipleship needs to happen in the context of a visible and situated community. The people of God also play an indispensable role in discipleship. By people of God, I am not referring to all Christians everywhere but specifically to local church families.

In the New Testament the local church is portrayed as a family, as "the household of God" (1 Tim. 3:15). Through the regenerating work of the Holy Spirit, we become members of the family of God, which is manifested in the local church. This family consists of spiritual fathers and mothers and brothers and sisters who care for and shape one another. For Christians, formation happens in the context of a family—both nuclear and ecclesial. We are a part of a family that forms.

The danger of de-emphasizing the role of local church families in our formation is that we communicate that discipleship is pursued through spiritual orphanhood. Discipleship that happens primarily outside of the local church is discipleship that happens primarily outside of the context of the spiritual family. This kind of discipleship means we tend to act as if we are spiritual orphans, not adopted sons and daughters.

Spiritual orphans do not have spiritual fathers and mothers to care for them. They do not have spiritual siblings to encourage them. They do not have their own spiritual sons and daughters to grow in the faith. In this setting, spiritual orphans learn only to look out for themselves because they do not have a family to consider. The good of the one is more important than the good of the whole. The growth of the one is more important than the growth of the whole. Spiritual orphans become primarily concerned with their own formation, not the formation of the whole family. They have no need to consider the rest of the family, just themselves. Often spiritual orphans are interested in growing in a knowledge of God but not a love of neighbor (1 Cor. 13:2).

However, when we root deep discipleship in the local church, there are no spiritual orphans. The local church is living out the gospel truth that we are no longer orphans, but we are now sons and daughters who are growing into spiritual adults. In the local church the formation of the whole person and the whole family matters. Each member of the family is indispensable to the growth of the rest of the family. The family members need one another.

One of the primary characteristics of this family is that they care for one another as much as they care for themselves. This is a key characteristic of holistic discipleship: that we are to pursue, not just our own formation, but the formation of the whole family. What would it look like for you to create a culture where everyone, in love and charity, pursued not just their own formation but also the formation of the household? Holistic disciples are not only seeking their own spiritual health but the spiritual health of the whole family. They understand that the health of the family is essential to their own wholeness.

Jesus alludes to this virtue in Luke 10:27: "You shall love the Lord your God with all your heart and with all your soul and with all your strength and with all your mind, and your neighbor as yourself." Notice what he is saying here. Though he is not speaking specifically of the local church, he is showing us that the faith is inherently communal. Love of God and love of self by itself is not whole. We are called to love God, self, and neighbor. Our closest neighbors are those in our own house and in our own spiritual house—the local church.

When discipleship is removed from the context of God's people, it can tend to be characterized by competition or comparison. For example, if your primary formation came in the form of an academic environment, a nonprofit, or an online platform, there can tend to be competition among participants. There is competition for grades, feedback, the attention of teachers, and perhaps for opportunities, like a job, after the course is over. In all likelihood you will not know most of your classmates five to ten years from now, so it is easy not to be invested in their own spiritual growth. Spiritual orphans see other spiritual orphans as competition, not as family. In discipleship environments like this, we are implicitly formed into the belief that our formation matters more than the formation of others. This is an intensely individualistic way of thinking about discipleship. We have no invested interest in seeing others growing in holistic formation; our sole investment is in our own growth, and anyone who gets in the way of that is seen as a threat to our own development.

The New Testament teaches us that we are supposed to view our church as a family in a special sense, which means that our discipleship is motivated by love for God and one another, not competition. We are to seek one another's interests, not just our own (Phil. 2:3). The church is marked by a familial type of love, a love that goes deeper than biological family. The church is to "love one another with brotherly affection. Outdo one another in showing honor" (Rom. 12:10). The Thessalonians are encouraged in this virtue as well: "Now concerning brotherly love you have no need for anyone to write to you, for you yourselves have been taught by God to love one another" (1 Thess. 4:9). The author of Hebrews contends, "Let brotherly love continue" (Heb. 13:1). Peter encourages Christians to continue to pursue "godliness with brotherly affection, and brotherly affection with love" (2 Pet. 1:7). Discipleship in the local church is meant to cultivate brotherly and sisterly, fatherly and motherly, love among members of the same household. Discipleship that happens in the context of the spiritual family is healthier than discipleship that happens in the context of a spiritual orphanage. When we pursue holisitic discipleship in the local church, we are as invested in one another's growth as much as we are invested in our own.

Discipleship is not meant to be characterized by competition but by charity, the kind of charity that should characterize a healthy family. A lot changes when the people you are learning alongside are not just classmates, online avatars, or Twitter handles but members of the same body. When we connect discipleship to the local church, we are highlighting the theological truths that all of us are adopted sons and daughters, that no son's or daughter's growth is more important than the others, and that we need one another in order to grow as a healthy family.

So, what does it look like to pursue charity, not competition, with the people of God? Discipleship in a family-like environment is meant to produce a familial kind of love for one another. In the local church we are not trying to create isolated disciples but members of a household.

At The Village Church, I helped start a discipleship environment called the Training Program. It is a one-year, intense discipleship environment in the context of the local church. The students write doctrinal statements, read huge portions of Scripture, memorize large passages, participate in spiritual disciplines, and more. It is one of the more spiritually intense environments I have seen in the local church.

One of my concerns when we created this environment was making sure students interacted through the lens of charity—not competition. I wanted to make sure they saw one another as members of the same family, who were meant to build up one another, not see one another as competition. It would be easy to see spiritual competition in an environment like this. In light of that, and because this is a local church discipleship environment, I make charity, or familial love, a requirement of each participant. We include the following paragraph in the syllabus:

> The greatest of these is love (1 Cor. 13:13). Disciples of Jesus are called to be marked by their love for God and their love for neighbor. Training Program participants are going to be called to make progress in their walk with Christ, and also to demonstrate a posture of love towards God and one another. Discipleship is never an individual task, but by definition is community oriented. While communal discipleship presents many challenges, it also presents many opportunities for us to be charitable with one another. A

charitable and loving spirit is required of all
Training Program participants.

Something I have seen over and over again in discipleship environments outside the church is student frustration when other participants are in a different place in their spiritual formation journey. For example, in a seminary classroom, more advanced students may get frustrated when less advanced students are monopolizing the classroom time by asking elementary questions. Perhaps the professor has covered this material over and over again, but the same student keeps asking basic questions. It would be easy for other students to view that student, and their questions, as a threat to their continual growth. In fact, they have paid to be there, they don't know this other student very well, and it's easy to understand why they could get frustrated. Or sometimes the opposite is true, more elementary students can get frustrated when the conversation is too advanced for them to keep up. After all, they are here to be formed and have no investment in seeing others in the class formed. I have seen this happen over and over again, not just in academic environments but in campus ministries and Bible studies as well.

But in the context of our spiritual family, we have no need to compare ourselves with one another but to encourage one another. For example, in the local church we can expect people to be at all kinds of different levels of maturity—just like different members of a family. There are spiritual fathers and sons, spiritual daughters and mothers. Some may have been walking with the Lord for decades and others for weeks. Some may have advanced degrees from seminaries, and others may not know the first thing about how to study their Bible.

So, how do you have all members of the family pursuing maturity together, without falling back into the habits of comparison, competition, and frustration? We need to see one another as family. What if more mature saints viewed themselves as fathers and mothers who are meant to encourage and exhort younger believers as if they were their own sons and daughters? What if sons and daughters championed the growth and development of their more mature fathers and mothers? What if we were as invested in one another's growth as we are invested in our own? What if the holistic discipleship of others mattered as much as our own? What if that is a part of holistic discipleship?

I once had a student named David in a discipleship environment in the church. He had a ThM and was considering doctoral work in ecclesiology. In the same class I also had a student named Samantha, a mother of five, with no formal theological training. David was thrilled and excited to be in the class, but Samantha was a bit nervous. At the beginning of the class, we introduced the importance of charity, as noted above, and that each participant needed to have a personal interest in the growth of others in the class, not just their own growth. When we were spending time on complex theological issues that David was just eating up, I could tell that Samantha was a bit lost and confused. She could have responded by checking out, maybe by not coming back, or just by expressing frustration that she was not personally benefitting from the discussion. Instead, she responded by encouraging him, by pressing into the conversation, and by expressing thanksgiving to God that he was growing David. She was as excited about his formation as she was her own. This is how spiritual siblings should treat one another! In the local church we celebrate the growth of our brothers and sisters because it makes the whole family healthier.

The opposite was true as well. When we were spending time on some more simple, elementary issues, David could have been frustrated because he had covered these things before, but instead he rejoiced in the growth of his sister. They both realized that they are family. What does a mother do when she sees her son crawl for the first time? She rejoices! It is always a joy to see a family member mature. What does a daughter do when she sees her father learn something new? She rejoices! It is always a joy to see older family members continue to learn. This is how healthy churches and holistic discipleship cultures are sustained in the local church.

A loving family environment is essential to deep discipleship. It is where newer and younger brothers and sisters are able to ask simple questions, and their siblings celebrate their growth. It's a place where older, more mature brothers and sisters are able to grow and mature as fast as the Spirit will allow them, and the younger siblings are able to look up to their older siblings and celebrate what God is doing in their lives.

I cannot emphasize how important this is. A culture of charity, curated in the local church, where we pursue the love and knowledge of God and neighbor together, is what makes discipleship inside the context of the local church qualitatively better than discipleship outside the local church. In the local church we are reminded that we are not spiritual orphans but adopted sons and daughters, part of the whole family of God. Only the whole family can create whole disciples.

Purpose

The local church is the visible and situated (place), adopted family of God (people), that is being equipped for mission and Christlikeness (purpose). Deep discipleship in the local church is different because the purpose of the church is different from any other institution on the planet. In his letter to the Ephesians, we can get some insight into Paul's hope and purpose for local churches:

> And he gave the apostles, the prophets, the evangelists, the shepherds and teachers, to equip the saints for the work of ministry, for building up the body of Christ, until we all attain to the unity of the faith and of the

knowledge of the Son of God, to mature man-
hood, to the measure of the stature of the fullness of Christ, so that we may no longer be
children, tossed to and fro by the waves and
carried about by every wind of doctrine, by
human cunning, by craftiness in deceitful
schemes. Rather, speaking the truth in love,
we are to grow up in every way into him who
is the head, into Christ, from whom the whole
body, joined and held together by every joint
with which it is equipped, when each part is
working properly, makes the body grow so
that it builds itself up in love. (Eph. 4:11–16)

While there is a lot to unpack here, I want to focus on two
things: mission and Christlikeness—those are the purposes of
the church. Discipleship in the local church is qualitatively different because we are pursuing mission and Christlikeness, a
purposes unique to the local church.

What is Jesus doing right now? According to Ephesians 4,
Jesus is ascended in the heavens, and he is building and gift-
ing his church for greater mission and unity. He is giving the
church leaders, who equip all the saints for ministry, for the
purpose of the whole family being built up in maturity. If that
is what Jesus' mission is, then that is the local church's mission as well. The central point of this passage is that Jesus is
distributing gifts to the church to unite them in mission and

THE CHURCH: WHERE WHOLE DISCIPLES ARE FORMED

build them up in maturity.[2] Ephesians 4 is not just about what the church should be doing but about what Jesus is doing for and through his church. He is giving his church leaders so that the whole church may be equipped for ministry. Our purpose should be aligned with his purpose.

One trend that is common in the church is an expert-amateur divide. There are the teachers and shepherds, and then there are the saints. The divide between the experts and amateurs is easily seen when the experts—those who are employed by the church—think their job is to do ministry *for* the saints not *with* the saints. They are on the stage, writing curriculum, holding a microphones, and leading ministries. This looks like pastors who read and teach the Bible in such a way that their congregation thinks, *I can never read the Bible like that.* This looks like worship leaders who are more interested in putting on a worship performance for an audience than they are interested in calling the congregation into greater participation. The experts are perceived to be the ones who really do the work of ministry. Experts are seen to have some kind of talent, gift, or skill set that sets them apart from the rest of the congregation—they are the spiritually elite.

Meanwhile, there is also a group of people who perceive themselves to be the amateurs. Rarely are they given the opportunity to do ministry, but they passively receive the ministry

---

2. Harold W. Hoehner, *Ephesians: An Exegetical Commentary* (Grand Rapids: Baker Academic, 2002), 538.

done by the experts. Amateurs are the beneficiaries of the labors of ministry of the experts. The amateurs get to sit in the audience, consuming from the work of the experts.

Too often "ministry experts" enjoy the distance between themselves and the congregation of "amateurs." They enjoy being seen as the experts, and they have little incentive to bridge the gap, so instead they make the gap greater. But that is not what Paul outlines as the purpose of the church: to equip the saints for the work of ministry. Ministers and pastors and leaders aren't called to do all the ministry *for* the congregation but to serve and prepare the congregation so the so-called amateurs can carry out the work of the ministry.

In other words, truly great teachers do not create distance between themselves and their students; they are set on removing that distance by helping their students learn. Likewise, students do not only want to observe great teachers; they want to learn so they can participate. Leaders in the church do not create distance between themselves and the people they are leading—they equip them for the work of ministry. Ephesians 4 is not calling teachers, ministers, and pastors who feel called to do the work of ministry *for* the church but *with* the church.

God is not interested in creating an audience; he wants participants. Paul is insistent that one of the main purposes of the church is to invite all people into the work of ministry— not reserve it for a select few. In the church there is not a group of people who do ministry and a separate group of people who receive the work of ministry. All members of the family are called to do the work ministry, and all members of the family are called to receive the ministry of others. We are one body with many members (1 Cor 12:12).

That means leaders are supposed to bridge the gap. Churches that want to create a culture of deep discipleship call on everybody to participate. They want to get all people—every single member—involved in the mission of building up the body of Christ.

The second purpose outlined for the church is that all members are being called to maturity—growing in Christlikeness. This may be one of the biggest gaps I currently see in ministry philosophies. As I have already outlined, most maturing happens outside of the family of God. Paul insists that the purpose of the local church is not only to equip the saints for ministry but to lead them into growth in their faith and knowledge of the Son of God (maturity) "to the measure of the stature of the fullness of Christ" (Eph. 4:13). God's goal for Christ's body, and for each individual member, is continual maturation into the image of Christ. No other organization shares that same purpose. Churchless discipleship is purposeless discipleship.

Deep discipleship in the church is to help you and the people you lead learn God's will for your life. God's will for your life is Christlikeness. There is no other corporate body in the world, other than the local church, that has been given that mission. The local church is the people of God, who in all kinds of different contexts and situations, are equipping and pointing people to the fullness of maturity in Christ. If the end of discipleship is Christlikeness, then all of our ministry efforts should be aiming people toward that end. F. F. Bruce highlights this as he argues, "The glorified Christ provides the standard at which his people are to aim: the corporate Christ cannot be content to fall short of the perfection of the personal Christ."[3] The local church is the family that is growing up in Christ. What Paul is aiming for in Ephesians is that gifted people in the church have the responsibility of helping others find and use their gifts for the building up of the body of Christ. That process will continue until all believers mature into the measure of the fullness of Christ.[4] The purpose of the local church is to point people to that end and equip them on that journey. The primary purpose of discipleship in the local church is maturing in Christ together.

Presence

The local church is the visible and situated (place), adopted family of God (people), that is being equipped for mission and Christlikeness (purpose), through the indwelling and empowering ministry of the Holy Spirit (presence).

---

3. F. F. Bruce, *The Epistle to the Ephesians: A Verse-by-Verse Exposition* (Grand Rapids: Fleming H. Revell Company, 1961), 87–88.
4. Hoehner, *Ephesians*, 551.

Paul reminds the local church at Corinth of this important truth. He asks them, "Do you not know that you are God's temple and that God's Spirit dwells in you?" (1 Cor. 3:16). Paul is speaking specifically to the local church, as indicated by the plural *you*, not just individual believers. Further, the plural *you* indicates that Paul is not referring to individual believers but to the corporate body, the church. In this instance, he calls them "God's temple." Paul uses a word to refer specifically not to the entire temple complex but to the actual sanctuary—the presence of God. In the Old Covenant God's presence resided in the temple, but now he resides in his church.

Similarly, in Ephesians 2:21, the church is referred to as the temple, and in 1 Peter 2:5 the church is "a spiritual house." Paul's theology of the empowering presence of God guides his philosophy of ministry in the local church. He is saying that the local church is indwelt by God himself. The local church needs to be reminded that we are indwelt and empowered by the presence of God. At the end of the day, it does not matter what your strategy and structure are if you are not relying on and celebrating the presence of God in the local church.

Ministry in the local church is fundamentally different because it is fueled and empowered by the presence of God. At the end of the day, there is no philosophy of ministry that is better than the presence of God.

The presence of God is better than a ministry philosophy when it comes to forming holistic disciples. In God's presence we are formed into whole people. God's presence is certainly not limited to the local church, but God is particularly present with his people when they gather. He is present with us as we sing, preach, and celebrate the Lord's Table and baptism. The presence of God is better than any ministry strategy, and the local church is full of the presence of God.

Conclusion

The local church is uniquely appointed, in God's divine providence and wisdom, to make disciples. I certainly believe local churches should collaborate with one another and with other organizations as they seek to participate in the mission of God, but collaboration is not delegation. The local church cannot delegate discipleship to others. I don't believe any local church sets out to delegate their discipleship responsibilities of their church—I believe it happens over time. But it is time for the church to pick up the mantle as the primary discipleship engine of the family of God. That is what Jesus wants us to do.

Main Ideas

1. Churchless discipleship is aimless discipleship.

2. The church is called to make disciples, and it is time for us to stop delegating our responsibility. Other organizations can come alongside the church, but they can never replace the church.

3. The local church is the visible and situated adopted family of God that is being equipped for mission and Christlikeness through the indwelling and empowering of the Holy Spirit.

Questions for Discussion

1. Do you agree that the local church should be the primary vehicle for discipleship? Why or why not?

2. Do you agree that, in large part, the local church has outsourced discipleship to parachurch organizations? If so, how have you seen that play out? What impact does that have on Christians and on churches?

3. Has your church taken up its mantle as the primary discipleship vehicle of its members, or has it outsourced discipleship to other organizations?

To-Do List

1. Have each person discussing the book share his or her discipleship journey—whether it has happened primarily in the local church or in organizations outside the local church.

2. Play out together the imagine scenario on pages 51–52. What would it take for your church to meet a nonbeliever and provide opportunities for training him to eventually become the next lead pastor in twenty years?

3. Pull out the list of ideas you began to jot down after reading and discussing the introduction. Try refining them in light of the last two chapters. How might your proposed treatment plan for the church's discipleship disease be implemented in your church?

CHAPTER 3

Space: Where Does Discipleship Happen in the Church?

We have given an either/or answer to a both/and question. Does your church primarily make disciples through small groups or through Sunday school? At our church we had basically abandoned Christian education and adopted a philosophy of ministry that relied almost entirely on small groups. We had a lot of environments that had the highest stated purpose of community and almost no environments where the highest stated value was learning.

I had a hard time with that approach because, while community is an indispensable element of discipleship, so is learning, and we were realizing that while small groups are great at a lot of things, they are not great at creating learning outcomes.

I do not think our church is unique in that. Most churches either have small groups or they have Sunday school; few churches have both. And the ones that do often do not see both as indispensable. What about your church? Have you given an either/or answer to a both/and question? If your church has an either/or approach, you are probably creating either/or disciples—disciples who are in community but lack discipleship outcomes related to learning, or who are learning but lack the kind of community that is indispensable to the Christian life.

The local church is the primary context in which Christ invites his followers to be shaped into holistic disciples. It is the primary context where his disciples are invited to step into the inexhaustible depths and riches of knowing and loving God. But we must get more specific than that. *How* does the local church actually shape and form disciples? What are some sustainable and effective strategies that we can implement to form holistic disciples? We cannot expect to form whole, deep disciples if we do not implement a holistic strategy.

The first question is the question of space. We have already said that deep discipleship should happen in the local church, but where in the local church? What ministry spaces do you have that you can use in order to form holistic disciples in your church?

Some churches believe formation primarily happens in the context of learning environments. These churches will tend to be programmatic and event driven and will implement environments like Sunday school. Other churches believe holistic formation happens primarily in the context of community. Churches like this will primarily invite disciples into environments like small groups, home groups, or missional communities. What kinds of environments does your church need to adopt in order to form holistic disciples? Answering this question is essential because creating healthy and vibrant spaces for discipleship is one of the main contributing factors to people growing in Christ. One question local churches ask is, "Where *can* we make disciples?," but the better question is, "Where *should* we make disciples?"

Discipleship Inventory

I think a great exercise for every church or ministry is to consider what spaces they are making for discipleship. Here are three questions that will help you evaluate your discipleship spaces: First, what spaces does your church have for discipleship? Take a quick stock of all environments that are available for your people to learn and grow in the Christian life. You have the weekly gathering, where the Word of God is proclaimed, sung, and prayed. You likely have spaces for kids to be trained and discipled in a manner that is age appropriate. You probably have a baptism class, maybe a next-steps class, and a membership class. A lot of churches have some kind of recovery environment, which provides a safe environment to confess sin and experience redemption. Does your church have group environments or classes to help equip and disciple adult believers? Take time to take stock of these spaces and consider: *What are these environments accomplishing in our discipleship pathway?* Maybe write down two or three words that each specific space contributes. What is it, exactly, that those spaces are accomplishing that no other ministry can accomplish?

Second, are these spaces functional or dysfunctional? What would it look like for you to bring health and functionality to dysfunctional spaces? Would it be better to simply eliminate those spaces altogether?

Third, what spaces are missing in your discipleship pathway, and what would those spaces accomplish? When you find yourself dreaming about adding ministry spaces, what are those? Would you add a residency, an internship, a training environment on how to read the Bible? What is missing that you would like to see added to your ministry spaces? What do you want this space to add that other discipleship environments cannot add by themselves?

After this exercise you will categorize all of your ministry spaces into the following headers:

- Essential and Functional (We have it, we
  need it, and it's working.)

- Nonessential and Functional (We have it, and it's working, but we do not need it.)
- Essential and Dysfunctional (We have it, and we need it, but it is broken.)
- Nonessential and Dysfunctional (We have it, but it is broken, and we do not need it.)
- Essential and Nonexistent (We need it, but we do not have it.)

I think this should be a regular practice for all of us in ministry because it constantly forces us to triage and ask hard questions about what we need to keep, cut, fix, and add to our ministry spaces.

This is not a chapter about all ministry spaces but about educational spaces in particular. Over the past several years many churches have begun adopting discipleship spaces that have the highest stated value of community while eliminating spaces that have the highest stated value of learning. Put simply, many churches are abandoning Sunday school and adopting groups. We have given an either/or answer to a both/and question. I can understand this trend because community is an absolutely indispensable element of growing healthy disciples in the local church. However, in this chapter I want to advocate that, if we want to make deep disciples, we also need to have spaces in the local church in which learning, in the context of community, is the highest stated value. This is ultimately a chapter arguing for the retrieval of Christian education in the local church.

A comment I hear over and over again in various discipleship environments is, "Why has nobody told me this before?" I hate hearing this. I remember one young woman by the name of Sarah. She had been a part of several healthy local churches as her job moved her around the country; she participated in various ministries through leading and volunteering; and eventually she got involved in one of the classes we were offering at The Village Church. She would often find me after class and through tears ask, "Why has nobody told me these things before?" She would comment that the things she was learning were so foundational that she had no idea how she had spent so much time in church without knowing these basic truths. Other times she would say, "If these things are true, then everybody needs to know them. How can we get this stuff to more people?" She would often make comments like this after classes on fairly robust theological topics like Trinitarianism or Christology. She had never been at a church that offered her the opportunity to learn the deep truths of the Christian faith in the context of the local church. She later told me that she was grateful for all the ministry opportunities that led her into healthy community, that they were absolutely indispensable to her spiritual vitality. But she lamented that it took so long for her to learn the basics of the faith. Commenting on her spiritual journey, she said, "I felt known by people, but I'm not sure I knew my faith." Sarah had been formed by an either/or church and had become an either/or disciple.

I've had that conversation, and conversations like it, numerous times. In our cultural moment it is so important for the church to be a place of belonging, a place where, as discussed in the previous chapter, we can enjoy familial relationships with others. A huge threat to healthy discipleship is isolation, and the church has the opportunity to offer real community, especially with the loneliness epidemic that plagues the West. It is almost impossible to overstate the importance of community in the Christian life. In an era in which so much of our world is built around the autonomous self and self-determinism, the church must testify to the importance of community for the Christian life.

Despite this trend, I want to advocate strongly for Christian education in the life of the local church. I want to state this clearly: community is indispensable to discipleship, but community is not discipleship. We cannot be disciples of Christ outside the context of community. However, we can be in community that is not teaching us to be disciples of Christ. Just because we get people into community does not mean we are discipling them. In other words, it is not enough to connect people to community; it must be a community that is committed to learning the way of Jesus together. It must be a community that learns.

We must retrieve education-driven discipleship spaces in the local church in order to form whole disciples. Discipleship is not just knowing and being known by others but also knowing God.

Christian education has fallen on hard times in the local church. The reality is we have relied heavily on community-driven spaces to accomplish things that only learning spaces can, and we are paying a steep price. Without a doubt, Christian education had a heyday in a lot of local churches. Whether it was traditional Sunday school, Wednesday night or Sunday night services, or a weekly Bible study, a lot of churches used to operate primarily around a mind-set of Christian education. While there are still many churches that have spaces for Christian education, there has been a seismic shift over the past few decades toward a groups' mind-set. Somewhere along the way, education and equipping became a nice supplement to discipleship but not an essential practice.

This is unfortunate because to be a disciple is to be a learner. Disciples are learning the way of Jesus. One of the most basic definitions of discipleship is found in the Great Commission: "All authority in heaven and on earth has been given to me. Go therefore and make disciples of all nations, baptizing them in the name of the Father and of the Son and of the Holy Spirit, *teaching them to observe all that I have commanded you*. And behold, I am with you always, to the end of the age" (Matt 28:18–20, emphasis added). According to Jesus, discipleship is all about learning and teaching; it centers on being taught and becoming a teacher. To disciple means to make students of, bring to school, educate, mentor, apprentice.[1] How can our members follow the way of Jesus if we do not teach them?

For Jesus, a disciple is someone who has received the identity of the Triune God through baptism and who follows the teaching of Christ through obedience. One of the greatest challenges the church faces today is that we believe discipleship ends with conversion. Our discipleship model is conversion and community; we have removed the concept of learning and growing from the equation and, therefore, we have largely removed spaces where learning can happen. Conversion is not the touchdown of the Christian life; it is the kickoff. Adoption into the family is not the end of life; it is the beginning.

The tragic irony of the demise of Christian education is that it is happening at precisely the wrong time. Study after study shows that Christians do not know their Bible, the basics of the faith, or how to practice spiritual disciplines. We are basically illiterate when it comes to the Christian faith, yet we are adopting philosophies of ministry that de-emphasize the importance of learning for the Christian life. For some reason, we have grown skeptical of learning and education in the church. This is unfortunate, given the overwhelming evidence

---

1. Frederick Dale Bruner, *Matthew: A Commentary: The Churchbook, Matthew 13–28*, Rev., Expanded ed., vol. 2 (Grand Rapids, MI: Eerdmans, 2007), 815.

that what is lacking in our discipleship is basic biblical and theological literacy. It's tragic that at the moment the church is struggling with deep discipleship, many ministry models have decidedly moved away from learning environments in the church.

Disciples who are in community but are not learning run the risk of loving their neighbor but not God. Disciples who are learning but who are not in community run the risk of loving God but not their neighbor. Disciples who are both learning and in community have the opportunity of being people who love God and neighbor.

Discipleship Spaces

So, what spaces does a church need to have in order to cultivate discipleship environments that form people into holistic disciples of Christ? We need to retrieve spaces that are dedicated to learning and implement them alongside, not in place of, our spaces that are committed to community. A mistake we make is assuming that one of these tools can accomplish both tasks. It is time for us to admit that we need two tools, not one. In community-driven spaces learning should happen. In learning-driven spaces community should happen. A culture of deep discipleship is birthed in a local church that has spaces where learning is the highest stated value and spaces where community is the highest stated value.

Before we look closer at discipleship spaces, it is important to point out that the primary space where Christ builds his church is in the weekend gathering. I believe any church that desires to create a culture of holistic discipleship needs to have a high view of how God corporately shapes and forms his people through the preached Word and corporate worship. Unfortunately, one trend in ministry is to discount the weekly gathering, which can be seen in less frequent attendance and by churches neglecting to meet. The author of Hebrews reminds us of the importance of gathering together for fellowship and proclamation of the gospel: "And let us consider how to stir up one another to love and good works, not neglecting to meet together, as is the habit of some, but encouraging one another, and all the more as you see the Day drawing near" (Heb. 10:24–25). The church is formed through the preached Word, the regular administration of the ordinances, and fellowship with the saints.

Some recent research suggests that even the most committed Christians will attend church on an average of two times per month—roughly 50 percent of the time. It is absolutely impossible to create a culture of holistic disciples if they only come to church twenty-six times a year. The fastest way to disrupt a journey of deep discipleship is to forsake regularly gathering together with the church.

The weekly gathering is the long game of deep discipleship. It does not matter what your philosophy of ministry is if people are not regularly being formed in the gathering. It does not matter how many community groups people are in, how many Bible studies or classes they participate in, or how many books they read if they are not gathering regularly with the whole church body. In the weekly gathering we come together to proclaim the good news to one another, to sing praise to our Triune God, to sit under the ministry of the Word, and to participate in the ordinances. Perhaps nothing is more formative than a few decades of regular church attendance. In the spring of 2020 the church was reminded of this truth as the COVID-19 virus forced many churches across the globe to postpone weekly gatherings and adopt virtual strategies of communication.

Yet the weekly gathering is not enough. We are always being discipled. We need to adopt a philosophy of ministry that shapes people seven days a week, not just one or two. We cannot assume that just because people are hearing the gospel on the weekends, they are not being formed by other forces every other day of the week. If we get them for two hours on Sunday, but Netflix gets them four hours every day, we are going to lose that battle every time. We need to develop and implement a philosophy of ministry that forms people every day, not just one or two days per week.

In addition to our weekly gathering, one discipleship space we reintroduced into the life of our church is men's and women's Bible studies. These studies are designed to go line by line through books of the Bible. Discipleship spaces like Bible studies are important because, in an increasingly biblically illiterate church, we have to model responsible ways of reading and teaching the Bible. We also believe in the importance of single-gender learning environments. This allowed us to raise up men and women who have the gift of teaching and give them opportunities to use their gift for the good of the body.

Another discipleship space we implemented is core classes—three particular classes dedicated to the essentials of the faith. These were designed to be accessible to nonbelievers or new believers and taught in such a way as to invite people into a conversation around the basics of their faith. We introduced these environments because we wanted everyone at our church to be able to have conversations about their faith in a relational context.

We also implemented a one-year discipleship Training Program, which I mentioned earlier. This program is designed to take people through the story of the Bible and introduce them to basic Christian beliefs and spiritual habits. The students are asked to write doctrinal statements, memorize Scripture, and recite the story of the Bible in twenty minutes. They read primary sources like Athanasius, Augustine, Calvin, and others. We were even able to establish relationships with local seminaries so that we can offer seminary credit to our participants if that's something they desire.

When we originally established the Training Program, we were praying for fifteen to twenty students each year. We thought that if we could train fifteen to twenty people at this intense level, we could transform the culture of the church over the next five to ten years. The first year we had 459 applicants.

When I saw how many people applied, I was not excited but terrified! How in the world were we going to accommodate that many participants in the first year of a program? We had to cap it somewhere, but we were able to accept 250 students in the first year. The pessimist in me thought we would not be able to retain a significant number of students. However, over the last five years we have more than a 90-percent retention ratio and more than a thousand graduates of the Training Program.

I share these numbers not to boast about our church but to demonstrate how desperate people in your church are to learn. We initially had twenty-five times the number of applicants I expected. Why not think your church has more eager learners than you expect as well? They want to be taught, they want to learn, they want depth, and they want you to establish environments like this that can take them deeper in their faith.

We also introduced a one-year residency program with two tracks—ministry and marketplace. The ministry track is designed to equip men and women for the roles of elder and deacon. The marketplace track is designed to help professionals see their vocation through the lens of the gospel and the glory of God.

As we were establishing these learning spaces, the most frequent question I received was: *Do these discipleship spaces that focus on learning compete with groups?* This is an understandable question. Their concern is that if they implement a classroom environment, they might be taking people away from group life. However, I believe the question reveals that many of us have adopted the either/or approach to discipleship. We learned that these spaces did not in any way compete with our community-driven spaces; they complemented them. Introducing learning spaces in the life of the church does not cannibalize group ministries; it strengthens them. We had two thousand people in classes or studies, 250 people in the Training Program, and twenty people in the residency program, and it did not hurt our group ministry but bolstered it.

We began to tell people they could opt out of group life and join a class or a study, and it was like a burden had been lifted. We told them we want them to be in community and we want them to learn, but they are responsible for determining what is best for them based on their own needs and desires.

Another regular question about the relationship between these two spaces is: Can we just have one space and accomplish both learning and community? Honestly, the answer is no. Allen Duty makes the point, "When churches offer *only* Sunday school classes *or* small groups, they are expecting the classroom to do what the living room does best, and the living room to do what the classroom does best."[2] Ideally, these two environments both exist in the life of the church. Yes, our community-based environments should have an element of learning. Yes, our education-based environments should have an element of fellowship. But it is ideal to have one environment with the highest stated purpose of learning and another with the highest stated purpose of community.

Should someone be in both environments? That depends. What is lacking in their holistic discipleship journey? Would they benefit most from a space dedicated to learning or a space dedicated to community? What is their life stage? Do they have kids? Are they married? When the local church offers both spaces, we are able to create environments that can help with different spiritual and life-stage needs.

In order to create deep disciples, we cannot lose our community-oriented discipleship spaces, but a lot of churches will have to retrieve spaces dedicated to Christian education. That is the main case I am making in this chapter: deep discipleship is equally oriented toward community and learning, and it is best for the church to offer two different spaces for those to occur. Since most churches are overly reliant on small groups as a discipleship strategy, they should work toward retrieving

---

2. Allen Duty, "Sunday School and Small Group: Friends Who Need No Reconciliation," *The Gospel Coalition* (blog), November 30, 2017, accessed December 20, 2019, https://www.thegospel coalition.org/article/sunday-school-and-small-group-friends-who -need-no-reconciliation.

learning spaces in the life of the church. We should not eliminate community-oriented discipleship spaces and replace them with learning-oriented spaces; we should recognize the need for both.

What Does a Learning Space Look Like?

What makes a learning space different from a community-oriented space? The best learning spaces in the local church will be both transformational and active. They need to be transformational because, even though learning is the highest stated goal, we are not merely aiming at the mind but the whole person. Christian education environments in the local church are aiming to transform the whole person, not just inform the mind. The goal is not simply to create smarter Christians but holy people.

Learning spaces also need to be active. We already have enough passive learning in the church, so we must introduce active learning spaces. Passive learning has the tendency to create passive disciples; active learning can create active disciples. Like the four legs of a table, active learning spaces have four important characteristics. Deep discipleship happens when we invite people to the four-legged table of active learning.

First, you should have participants working on something before the class. This may be reading an article or a chapter from a book or maybe some other kind of preclass work, like curriculum. This work should help students realize they need to grow. Too often Bible studies and curricula create a sense of satisfaction, not a sense of dissonance. You do not want the work to be so far over learners' heads that they are discouraged, but you want them to have a hunger for learning more.

Second, before you teach, your participants should gather together in smaller groups and discuss the preclass work. The preclass work and group discussion create a further sense of dissonance within the group. They are becoming a community of colearners on a journey toward truth. By following these two steps, your participants will grow in their awareness of what they do not know. You want them entering the teaching time not with a sense of what they know but what they do not know.

Third, your participants should then come to a large-group teaching environment. Here is your opportunity to teach them and relieve some of the dissonance. This is not a time for you to be a great teacher but for you to help them become great learners. The best teaching in these environments, different from a sermon, is dialogical. As you work through the material and help them grow in their understanding, you are fielding questions, showing them that you, the teacher, are also on the path of learning with them.

Fourth, your participants need to articulate what they have learned to someone else. This last step is essential for deep learning to happen. At the end of every week, ask them, "What did you learn, and to whom are you teaching it?" This is where real learning happens. Peter Drucker argues, "No one learns as much about a subject as the man who is forced to teach it, no one develops as much as the man who is trying to help others to develop themselves. Indeed, no one can develop himself unless he works on the development of others."[3] This is true discipleship. You need to give all participants the opportunity, the mandate, to have a conversation with their spouse, a coworker, a child, or a neighbor about what God is teaching them. All disciples make disciples, and active learning environments call every participant to, in some sense, be a teacher. The goal in active learning environments is not great teaching but deep learning. Deep learning happens through prework, group discussion, dialogical teaching, and articulation from the participant.

Deep discipleship is driven by the collaborative spaces of community and learning. When both of these discipleship spaces exist in the life of the church, they are both able to flourish as they are intended.

We had a big challenge as we reintegrated classes into the life of our church. For years we told people that discipleship happens primarily in small groups. They had been trained to think, *I must be in a small group, and I can be in a class.* We had prioritized small groups over classes, so our people prioritized community over learning. This was a mistake, and we had to

---

3. Peter F. Drucker, *Management* (New York: Harper Business, 2008), 428.

help our people unlearn it. We had to show people that small groups are not indispensable to discipleship—community is, but small groups are not. Likewise, classes are not indispensable to discipleship—learning is, but classes are not. All disciples are called into community and into learning. We had to retrain our people to realize that the virtue of being in community and the virtue of learning are more important than participating in a specific ministry. In other words, before we give people a discipleship process, we have to give them a discipleship picture. Disciples are learners. Disciples are in community. Giving people the next step is important, but it is not as important as showing them who they are supposed to be. In other words, we can't answer the question, "What am I supposed to do?," before we answer the more important question, "Who am I supposed to be?"

We cannot create holistic disciples when we believe we have to answer either/or to a both/and question. Learning-based environments and community-based environments do not compete with each other; they complement each other. If we have only community-driven spaces, we slowly begin to believe that community is the only pillar to discipleship. If we have only learning-driven spaces, we will slowly begin to believe that learning is the only pillar to discipleship. In short, we will develop an either/or approach to ministry instead of a both/and approach to ministry. A both/and approach will help your church develop deep disciples.

Main Ideas

1. Many churches have given an either/or answer to a both/and question. We've chosen community-oriented discipleship spaces over learning-oriented spaces, or learning-oriented spaces over community-oriented spaces. We should be choosing both.

2. Community is indispensable to discipleship, but community is not discipleship. We cannot be disciples of Christ outside the context of community. However, we can be in community that is not teaching us to be disciples of Christ.

3. Discipleship spaces where active learning is the highest stated value are indispensable to deep discipleship.

Questions for Discussion

1. Has your church chosen primarily community-oriented discipleship spaces or learning-oriented spaces? Why? How has this shaped the culture of your church?

2. Do you believe local churches should provide both kinds of discipleship spaces? Why or why not?

3. Define "active learning spaces." Does your church have any? If not, do you believe it should? What might these learning spaces look like in your church?

To-Do List

1. Work through the discipleship inventory on pages 80–81, placing each ministry at your church in one of these categories.

2. List all of the discipleship spaces in your church. How many are community-oriented, and how many are learning-oriented? List any of them that promote active learning. If they do not yet promote active learning, create a game plan for how to transition them to active learning environments.

3. Begin to brainstorm what it might look like down the road to change some of your discipleship spaces—removing some, adding others. Make a list of the different kinds of pushback you might receive and a plan to explain to the congregation why you are making these changes. Discuss how to gently shepherd your people into a culture of deep discipleship rather than forcing changes against their will.

CHAPTER 4

Scope: What Do Disciples Need?

I once worked at a church that had a few dozen-class offerings and several different studies for small groups to work through, along with a sermon discussion guide. This church was trying to create spaces that were equally committed to learning and community, which is a great place to start. There were some great offerings like parenting training, a class on the story of the Bible, a curriculum designed to help people be better stewards of their money, a recovery curriculum and corresponding groups, a young marrieds group, and more. All of these are great topics, and at different points in the life of a disciple perhaps some of these topics are indispensable.

However, I began to realize that the church staff itself didn't really know why we were offering one class and not another. Over the years, new offerings were provided, staff came and went, and we were left with what I call a Frankenstein philosophy of ministry. A Frankenstein philosophy of ministry is a ministry creation that is the result of a lot of ministry experiments that don't fit well together but end up being one big monster. Over the course of years, different things are added, taken away, and tweaked without considering the whole picture. Ministries were operating in silos, seeing only what mattered for their ministry. Just like an either/or approach to ministry, a Frankenstein philosophy of ministry cannot produce whole disciples. Usually this philosophy of ministry is birthed by asking the question, "What do disciples want?," instead of asking the better question, "What do disciples need?" Instead of asking the sheep what they want, good shepherds know what their sheep need.

Have you ever asked yourself the question, "How do all of these parts fit together?" For example, why offer a parenting class and not a class on Romans? Why offer a class on the doctrine of God and not a class on the doctrine of salvation? Should we do missional communities or small groups? Do those small groups work through their own curriculum, or should they discuss the sermon series? We realized we had never really sat down and decided why we were teaching and training toward a specific topic and how that topic related to other trainings.

Things were added over time, and we didn't really know why we should or shouldn't do things a certain way. We never really sat down to decide together what kind of curriculum we felt was indispensable—not just helpful—for discipleship.

If church leaders are confused about why we are teaching certain things and not others, then certainly the people we are teaching are equally, if not more, confused. We had never asked the question: *What is nice versus what is necessary?*

In my experience this is descriptive of most churches: we have good offerings, groups, and curricula for people, but we are unsure how each discipleship class, curriculum, or group relates to the others. We are unsure of how it all fits together. The most effective churches realize that the sum of their ministries is greater than the parts. When each ministry has an understanding of how it contributes to the whole, we are able to do more together than apart. Churches that do the hard work of asking and answering these hard questions have the greatest chance of producing and replicating deep disciples. All of these important questions fall under the question of scope: What do disciples need on their journey to holistic formation?

These questions are some of the most important questions one can answer in moving toward a holistic plan for discipleship in the local church. Answering them requires a great deal of courage because your answers will change your church. Some of the most important questions for a church to ask and answer are: "What do disciples need, and how can the church give it to them? What do we need to change in order to train, equip, and prepare our church to live as whole people? Is everything we are offering through groups, classes, and curriculum necessary to discipleship, or are we offering things that are nice?" All of these questions are ultimately questions about scope: What are the indispensable and unique characteristics of discipleship the church is responsible for embedding into the hearts, souls, minds, and bodies of their members? Scope is all about what is indispensable and necessary.

This is a question virtually every organization has already answered, whether they know it or not. For example, public school systems have to answer this question as they seek to develop responsible citizens. They have decided that topics like science, math, social studies, and physical education are appropriate topics for training young boys and girls. Gyms answer this question by helping people grow in their understanding of health, fitness, weight training, and diet. What you probably will not see is a schoolteacher training her students in scuba diving or a gym owner teaching his clients about basket weaving. But why? Because they have clearly defined their scope of responsibility. Every institution, including churches, has already answered—either intentionally or unintentionally—the question of scope. A gym knows what its members need, and a school knows what students needs, but does your church know what disciples need?

The Nonnegotiables of Discipleship

So here are some questions for you: Have you decided in what areas you must be training, equipping, and growing your people? What are the nonnegotiables of discipleship for you? Are you actually training and growing your people in these areas? The question of scope can be a ruthless question to answer because you may find out that a lot of your time, energy, and attention are going to good things but not great things.

I realized that in one church where I worked. I was given oversight of a ministry that had thirty-nine different course offerings with only 129 people involved. Each class had about three to six people involved. I began to see that all the time, energy, and attention given to nice-but-not-necessary things were contributing to a Frankenstein philosophy of ministry.

Once I became a Christian in college, I realized that this was a question most churches and Christian organizations had largely neglected. It wasn't that they were not teaching and training; it was that they had forgotten why they were teaching and training certain things. Most of the Christians I met had a deep love for the Lord but were largely untrained as it related to becoming deep disciples. They were the recipients and products of a Frankenstein approach to ministry. They knew the stories of the Bible but not the story of the Bible. They knew some secondary or tertiary Christian beliefs but not the basics of the faith. They knew that they were supposed to pray but did not understand how a larger picture of spiritual disciplines can form a whole disciple. Largely their discipleship, the kinds of people they were, was reflective of this Frankenstein approach to ministry. These disciples were products of an unclear and unintentional discipleship scope.

Every church must decide what the scope of discipleship is. If deep discipleship in the local church is focused on helping disciples grow deeper in fellowship with the infinitely beautiful and glorious God, what tools do disciples need on their journey?

Your scope represents what you think are the core competencies of discipleship. What is absolutely indispensable for your people to be learning and growing? What are the core competencies you believe every disciple should have? What are the absolute necessities a disciple of Jesus must study and learn in order to walk as a whole disciple of Christ? Most importantly, how can your church come alongside them and equip and train them for this work? I don't believe every church needs to answer this question the same way, but I do think there will be a lot of commonalities between churches.

Once you have decided what your scope is, start cutting away everything else; it is energy you do not need to be expending. Of course, do it slowly and with sensibility, but once you have decided a class or group is nice, not necessary, it is time for you to give it an exit plan. At least stop doing it until you have implemented discipleship spaces that train toward the core competencies you believe are essential to disciples. In other words, scope is your decision-making mechanism. Is it a part of your scope and core competencies? If yes, then fuel it. If not, then stop it. Scope is the solution to avoiding a Frankenstein philosophy of ministry.

How do you decide what your scope is? You need to think about what virtues, characteristics, or learning outcomes the disciples in your church must have. You cannot expect disciples to grow or be proficient in topics in which you are not providing training. In other words, train specifically and only toward the discipleship competencies you develop. We cannot expect people to learn what we are not teaching them.

As you think about the core competencies where you believe all disciples should develop proficiency, here are three areas I believe deserve your consideration. The three topics, or buckets, that I think present a comprehensive picture of discipleship are Bible, beliefs, and spiritual habits. A healthy disciple must be growing in the understanding of God's Word, founded on distinctively Christian beliefs and practicing spiritual disciplines. What does every disciple need? They need Scripture, doctrine, and spiritual habits.

The Bible must be at the center of the Christian life. It is God's Word, authoritative, inerrant, and sufficient for growing as a healthy disciple of Christ. Scripture is God's ordained means of revealing and giving himself to us.

Basic Christian beliefs are also indispensable for the Christian life. They help us know who God is, who we are, what the world is, and how we can be faithful participants in God's mission.

Spiritual habits help disciples train not just their heads but also their hearts and their bodies as disciples of Christ. Discipleship is not just growing to love God with our minds but with our whole selves. Spiritual habits help us become whole people.

These three categories together represent a comprehensive scope that provides both flexibility to teach topics that fit underneath these broader themes and clarity to make decisions of what is outside the discipleship scope of the local church.

Think of these three topics as ministry buckets that a lot of things can fit into, but not everything. Under the scope of the Bible you could offer:

- Equipping on how to read the Bible
- A class on the story of the Bible
- Studies on specific books of the Bible
- Old Testament and New Testament survey

Under basic beliefs you may decide to teach:

- Your church's doctrinal statement
- A historic creed or confession like the Apostles' Creed
- A class in systematic theology

In the bucket of spiritual habits, you could train toward:

- Sabbath
- Evangelism
- Prayer
- Healthy emotions
- Vocation and calling

There is still flexibility as you make decisions related to scope, but we should not confuse flexibility with a lack of clarity. The church has to be clear about what specific discipleship competencies you want them to be equipped in. Since this is your decision-making mechanism, you can begin to answer questions like: Should we offer a class on finances? Should we offer small-group curriculum on Romans? Should we offer classes specific to life stage, like singles, newlyweds, or parents? Every ministry decision related to discipleship is viewed through the lens of scope.

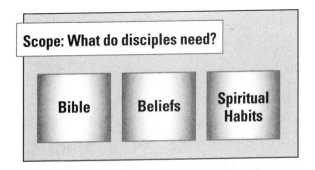

Therefore, the goal of scope is to help people grow in these three areas. Our entire philosophy of ministry should be guided by developing ministry environments that guide people into greater affection for Christ and the gospel through these three buckets. In other words, I am suggesting that once you have developed your scope—and perhaps you would take away from this list or add something else—this becomes your decision-making mechanism for ministry. Are we going to offer that training? Depends—does it fit inside our scope of discipleship? How are we going to organize our group life? Well, is it helping people grow in Scripture, Christian beliefs, or basic spiritual disciplines? Once you know what the core competencies of discipleship are, aim all of your efforts toward helping your people grow in them.

Bible

I want to spend some time advocating that this is a good and holistic scope for discipleship. Why should the Bible be part of the scope of discipleship? The Bible is at the center of the Christian life. It is impossible to be a follower of Christ without being a student of his Word. The Bible is God's inspired, authoritative, inerrant, and sufficient Word. Writing to Timothy, Paul highlights the centrality of Scripture for the Christian life when he argues: "All Scripture is breathed out by God and profitable for teaching, for reproof, for correction, and for training in righteousness, that the man of God may be complete, equipped for every good work" (2 Tim. 3:16–17).

The claim that the Bible is the breath of God means there is no substitute for Scripture in growing holistic disciples. The Bible is God's revelation of himself and his ongoing self-giving. In other words, Scripture is where God has made himself known, and it is where he continues to make himself known. Deep and holistic discipleship is birthed, sustained, and preserved in Scripture. Herman Bavinck highlights the centrality of Scripture for discipleship when he comments:

> In the Scriptures God daily comes to his people, not from afar but nearby. In it he reveals himself, from day to day, to believers in the fullness of his truth and grace. Through it he works his miracles of compassion and faithfulness. Scripture is the ongoing rapport between heaven and earth, between Christ and his church, between God and his children. It does not just tie us to the past; it binds us to the living Lord in the heavens. It is the living voice of God.[1]

---

1. Herman Bavinck, *Prolegomena*, ed. John Bolt, trans. John Vriend, vol. 1, *Reformed Dogmatics* (Grand Rapids: Baker Academic, 2003), 385.

The first act of churches that want to grow in deep fellowship and communion with God is to listen to what God says in Scripture.

We've already seen that one of the greatest challenges to discipleship is the biblical illiteracy that plagues the contemporary church. It is simply impossible to grow as a follower of Christ without being a student of his Word, yet we find that there are so few students of the Word. We lack deep disciples because we lack deep meditation on the Word. Biblical illiteracy is devastating to discipleship. The goal of Bible literacy is not simply biblical knowledge but participation. Knowledge of God's Word is meant to lead to participation in God's story. In other words, we should not be interested in people just doing better on Bible trivia; we should be interested in their ability to participate in God's story. I do not just want to get the story into people; I want to get people living into the story. Deep discipleship is about pursuing the kind of knowledge that transforms, not just informs. In Scripture, God is inviting us into deeper fellowship with himself and into greater participation in his mission.

Yet study after study suggests that the church has never been less familiar with our sacred text than we are today, even while we have never enjoyed more access to it. We have an abundance of biblical resources and a famine of biblical knowledge. You can't participate in a story you don't understand. If we don't know the story contained in the Bible from Genesis to Revelation—and by every indication we don't—how can we hope to participate in it?

James gives us a picture of what it means to both know and participate in the story of Scripture. He says: "Therefore put away all filthiness and rampant wickedness and receive with meekness the implanted word, which is able to save your souls. But be doers of the word, and not hearers only, deceiving yourselves. For if anyone is a hearer of the word and not a doer, he is like a man who looks intently at his natural face in a mirror. For he looks at himself and goes away and at once forgets what he was like" (James 1:21–24). Surely we need to be both hearers and doers of God's Word, but we can't expect to be doers until we have first been hearers.

Hearing God in his Word is a prerequisite to doing God's Word in our lives. The goal of biblical literacy is faithful participation in God's mission, to be both hearers and doers of God's Word. However, while the church suffers through a crisis of biblical illiteracy, we run the risk of being doers without first being hearers. If we send people to participate in God's mission, without knowing what his mission is, then we run the real risk of inventing our own mission. The discipleship outcome of Bible literacy is biblical participation in God's mission.

I imagine that almost everybody reading a book like this agrees with almost everything I have said so far. We are facing a crisis in biblical literacy. Check. We need to grow in our knowledge of the Bible, not just so we can know it better but so that we might participate in it. Check. In other words, most of us agree that as God has called us to lead in the church and to make disciples, the Bible needs to be at the center of what we are doing. We agree that the Bible is God's Word.

If we agree on all of this, then what is the point? My point is that it is not enough to agree with the doctrine of biblical authority if it is not impacting the way we do ministry and the kind of disciples we are making.

How is it that we agree on the Bible's authority, yet so many of our churches are biblically illiterate? Most of us have a doctrinal confession of biblical authority that does not line up with our application in ministry. You may think the Bible is at the center of your discipleship program, but it may not be. Having a statement on biblical authority on your website is futile if you are not practicing biblical authority in your ministry. The Bible is not an accessory in discipleship; it is a necessity. The canon is the curriculum of the Christian life. Only the whole Bible can make whole Christians.

What would it look like for the members of your church to know not just some of the stories in the Bible but the story of the Bible? What if your philosophy of ministry could help them become participants in that story and could help them learn how to invite others into that story as well? "Disciples need to learn how to inhabit the story of the Bible,"[2] claims Kevin Vanhoozer. If your church is not helping people know

---

2. Kevin J. Vanhoozer, *Hearers and Doers: A Pastor's Guide to Making Disciples through Scripture and Doctrine* (Bellingham, WA: Lexham Press, 2019), 112.

and participate in the true story of Scripture, their minds, hearts, and imaginations will be captivated by other, false stories. There is no greater tool for deep discipleship than encountering God in Scripture. He does the work through the Word. The Bible is not for the spiritually elite; it is for every disciple. As you are thinking about the scope of discipleship for your church, Scripture should be at the center. Without it deep discipleship is impossible.

Beliefs

The second core competency for whole disciples is a growing understanding and appreciation for Christian beliefs. Doctrine is for everybody. Basic Christian beliefs are the most practical thing the church can give disciples. Often theology is seen as an obstacle to discipleship, but it is actually the foundation of Christian living. The term *theology* comes from two Greek words: *theos*, meaning God, and *logos*, meaning Word. It basically translates as "words about God, or God's Word about himself." Is anything more practical than words about God? Is anything more important and practical than synthesizing and understanding what God has said about himself? I do not think there is. Doctrine and discipleship go hand in hand.

In many churches, theology has gained a reputation of being distant, impractical, and unimportant. I have even heard some pastors and churches say that doctrine gets in the way of true discipleship. Many people have seen doctrine divide and not heal, confuse and not guide. The truth is, I have seen that too. But that is not the fault of doctrine; it is the fault of people misusing doctrine.

When we see theology as unimportant for discipleship, it is not as if our people are adopting a doctrineless discipleship. If we fail to teach disciples how to believe like Christians, they will adopt other beliefs. Everyone is a theologian because everyone has words about God. Everyone has gone to seminary; the only question is whether we know it or not. The question for our churches and for the people we are discipling is: *Are we forming people who think and believe Christianly, or are we neglecting doctrine and letting the world form them into people who think and believe like the world?*

Basic Christian beliefs are essential for deep and holistic discipleship in the local church, and holistic disciples know they are theologians.

When did indoctrination become bad? Indoctrination happens almost everywhere. Songs, schools, books, movies, cable news, social media—literally everything is meant to indoctrinate us. Our people are being shaped and formed into certain ways of believing, and the local church must be the place where Christians are trained to believe like disciples of Christ.

One of the first things pilots are taught to do when flying a plane is to keep their eyes on the horizon. They are trained to set their eyes on the horizon because this will keep the plane from plummeting dangerously close to the ground, from ascending too quickly into the sky, or from tilting to the right or the left. Keeping your eyes on the horizon is the basic instinct of any pilot flying a plane.

But what happens when a pilot is unable to keep his eyes on the horizon? What happens when clouds, rain, snow, and darkness limit a pilot's ability to see? The instinct of most pilots is to trust their intuition and spatial orientation. In other words, they want to feel their way through their inability to see. Yet, all pilots are taught not to trust their intuition in moments like this because of spatial disorientation.

Spatial disorientation is the phenomenon of not being able to tell where your body—or plane, in this instance—is in space. In a sense, your instincts and feelings lie to you. In spatial disorientation you cannot tell where your body is in space, even though you think you can. You may feel right side up, but in reality you are upside down. Pilots are trained, if they can't see the horizon, to keep their eyes on the gauges—even and especially when it may feel like the plane is plummeting or ascending. By trusting their gauges, they are able to keep the plane on course and away from anything that could harm the plane and the passengers.

Think about how counterintuitive that is. Trusting the gauges requires an incredible amount of faith because at times it doesn't feel right. It feels disorienting, and it feels dangerous.

But when they trust the gauges and visibility is restored, they are flying right side up and in the right direction.

Doctrine is the gauges of the Christian life. It is what orients disciples in a disorienting world. When the church fails to give disciples theology, we are abandoning them to trust their intuition in the darkness of the world. We are telling them that they do not need to receive direction from anything else other than what they feel is right—and many of them are crashing. Misguided beliefs lead to a misguided life.

In 2018 Lifeway Research and Ligonier Ministries released a research project on "The State of Theology."[3] This research is meant to help local churches understand the current theological temperature of the church. The results are sobering.

The church is confused about who God is, what it means to be an image-bearer, who Christ is, what sin is, what salvation is, and much more. For example, we can see that evangelicals are largely confused about the person of Christ. When asked to agree or disagree with the statement "Jesus is the first and greatest being created by God," a fourth-century heresy known as Arianism, 78 percent of evangelicals agreed. The church is also largely confused about the exclusivity of Christ. When asked to agree or disagree that "God accepts the worship of all religions, including Christianity, Judaism, and Islam," 51 percent of evangelicals agreed. One final example: when asked to agree

---

3. "The State of Theology," The State of Theology, accessed April 7, 2020, https://thestateoftheology.com.

or disagree, "Everyone sins a little, but most people are good by nature," a heresy known as Pelagianism, 52 percent of evangelicals agreed.

These results are alarming, not only because evangelicals are getting questions wrong on a survey, but because these are the kinds of disciples that are being made in our churches.

When we see research like this, it is easy, as a pastor or leader, to assume it does not represent your church but the church down the street. We believe that while we could probably do a little bit better, but we also assume we are doing better than some other churches in town. This is the wrong instinct. Research like this gives all of us the opportunity to look in the mirror and realize that in our attempt to create doctrine-less disciples, we are actually creating doctrinally confused disciples. All disciples believe doctrine, just not always Christian doctrine. This research does not just reflect the church down the street; this research reflects your church. This is one reason basic Christian beliefs need to be included in your scope and core competencies for holistic discipleship. It is time for us to realize that our people are trusting their untrustworthy instincts, not the trustworthy gauges of Christian beliefs.

The lack of sound doctrine in the church has not always been the case. For centuries the church was led by creed, confession, and catechism. One of the ways forward for holistic disciples in the local church is a recovery of doctrinally motivated discipleship. Discipleship that is apathetic to doctrine, beliefs, and theology is not Christian discipleship.

Why is doctrine so important? It is important because of what it is—the pathway into deeper fellowship and joy with God. Our belief about who God is leads us deeper into communion with him, not further away from him. Doctrine is ultimately about love.

My wife, Macy, and I talk about this all the time. We have been married for twelve years, and I adore her. Nobody in the world has taught me more about God than she has. In fact, she was one of the first Christians I met. Let me tell you a little bit about her. She is in the technology industry; she is five feet four inches tall, and has beautiful brunette hair. One of the things I love the most about her is how artistic and creative she is. I love her more than anyone else in the world.

If you actually knew my wife, you would question how much I love her based on that description. My wife is actually in the marketing industry. She is five feet ten inches tall and has gorgeous blonde hair. She is not very artistic but is very athletic. Based on my inability to describe my wife accurately, you would wonder, *Does he really love his wife, or does he just say that he loves his wife?* You might wonder if I really knew her all that well. If I was regularly misdescribing, misunderstanding, and misrepresenting who Macy is, eventually you would begin to question my love for her. You would wonder how deep our relationship is when it appears that I don't even know her. We understand that knowing who someone is, knowing everything about them, and delighting in them are parts of loving them.

Doctrineless disciples cannot love God because they do not know him. We need to confront the idea that pervades evangelicalism that we can worship a God we do not know. As Jen Wilkin points out: "The heart cannot love what the mind does not know."[4]

Doctrine does not lead to displeasure but to delight. Knowledge of God leads us deeper into God, not further away from God. Knowing who my wife is, knowing all I can about her, leads to love. Similarly, knowing who God is, knowing all we can about him, leads disciples into deeper fellowship and love.

Paul highlights this in his letter to the Colossians: "And so, from the day we heard, we have not ceased to pray for you, asking that you may be filled with the knowledge of his will in all spiritual wisdom and understanding, so as to walk in a manner worthy of the Lord, fully pleasing to him: bearing fruit in every good work and increasing in the knowledge of God" (Col. 1:9–10). For Paul, holistic disciples are filled with, and are increasing in, the knowledge of God. Why? Because it is then, and only then, that they can walk in a manner worthy and pleasing to him. Knowledge of God leads to faithfulness

---

4. Jen Wilkin, *Women of the Word: How to Study the Bible with Both Our Hearts and Our Minds* (Wheaton, IL: Crossway, 2014).

and fruitfulness. We cannot be faithful and fruitful to a God we do not know.

Jeroslav Pelikan defines doctrine as "what the church believes, teaches, and confesses as it prays, suffers, serves, and obeys, celebrates, and awaits the coming of the Kingdom of God."[5] In other words, basic Christian beliefs guide the church into holistic discipleship in every season of life as we wait for the coming of the kingdom of God. It is the spectacles we put on in order to interpret the world around us. Kevin Vanhoozer says it this way: "Christians learn doctrine in order to participate more deeply, passionately, and truthfully in the drama of redemption."[6] If this is true, deep discipleship is dependent on doctrine, and churches that want to make deep disciples must guide their churches into faithful belief.

One reason many churches have moved away from the role of doctrine in discipleship is in response to the tendency to emphasize the wrong doctrines. Not all beliefs are the same—there are core beliefs and secondary beliefs. There are doctrines we hold with a closed hand and others we hold with an open hand. Sometimes churches become more known for openhanded, secondary doctrines than closehanded, core doctrines. The reason I think that is the case is that secondary

---

5. Jaroslav Pelikan, *Development of Christian Doctrine: Some Historical Prolegomena* (New Haven, CT: Yale University Press, 1969), 118.
6. Kevin J. Vanhoozer, *The Drama of Doctrine: A Canonical Linguistic Approach to Christian Doctrine* (Louisville, KY: Westminster John Knox, 2005), 107.

doctrines—like infant/believer baptism, continuationism/ cessationism, complementarianism/egalitarianism—are what separate some Christians from other Christians. Historically speaking, this makes sense. In a perceived culture and climate that is overtly Christian, a church's primary instinct is to distinguish itself from other churches, not the world. In other words, Baptists distinguish themselves from Presbyterians, Presbyterians distinguish themselves from Anglicans, and Anglicans distinguish themselves from free-church evangelicals. However, in an increasingly secular climate, Christians need to be less focused on what separates us from one another and more focused on what separates us from the world. What distinguishes Christians from the world is not secondary issues but primary issues, like Trinitarianism, creation, providence, and Christology.

While secondary issues are still important, they are not as important for holistic disciples as the foundational and primary issues. Yet sometimes we still major on the minors.

At a church I served, we were working through our membership material, and it struck me that the membership booklet had a three-page exposition on complementarianism and one bullet point on Trinitarianism. We were interested in making sure that our potential members understood our stance on men and women, but, at least according to appearance of the pamphlet, less interested in our potential members being Trinitarians. We were running the risk of admitting members who were clear in their understanding of complementarianism and confused in their understanding of Trinitarianism.

Part of reintroducing doctrine into the local church will be helping our church and our people do doctrinal triage. We need to know what matters most and why. For example, it does us no good to create a complementarian Unitarian. Even though I am a committed complementarian, I would far rather be in fellowship with a Trinitarian who is an egalitarian than a complementarian who is a Unitarian.

As we reintroduce doctrine into the life of the local church, we need to start with the essentials, not the nonessentials. Deep disciples want to meditate on the Triune Godhead; they want to consider the mystery of the incarnation and be captivated by the hope of the resurrection of the dead. When we start with the essentials, we are able to show more simply the pastoral nature of theology and how it aids the Christian life. Our churches will begin to see Trinitarianism as the foundation for all of the Christian life. They will see how union with Christ is perhaps the most pastorally helpful doctrine available to us. They will see how the doctrine of the atonement offers assurance to the anxious. Doctrine is deeply pastoral.

Let me give you an example of the pastoral nature of doctrine. There was a couple in one of my classes for several years. They had been involved in Bible studies for years and eventually entered our one-year discipleship Training Program. As we were making our way through the curriculum, we spent a week on creation and providence—that God creates and governs all things. This was a doctrine that, candidly, they really struggled with. It was challenging for them to see how a good God could create all things, govern all things, and be infinitely powerful yet still allow bad things to happen—a question many have struggled with for centuries. Shortly after that lecture they dealt with several tragic deaths in their family. The doctrine they thought was going to be a hindrance, instead, brought healing. If God is not sovereign, we cannot trust him in the storm; but if he is, then this doctrine is a sure and steady anchor for the soul in every season.

Doctrine did not hinder their fellowship with God; it invited them deeper into fellowship with God. It was the trustworthy gauge they could follow when their entire world was going through severe turbulence, leaving them disoriented. I have seen students find comfort in the sovereignty of God as they or loved ones face death. Others have been encouraged in their union with Christ in the midst of battling against sin. Some have taken refuge in the fatherhood of God while struggling with infertility. The future resurrection comforted one particular student as she endured round after round of chemotherapy treatment. She would sit in class, week after week, slowly losing her hair and weight, all while growing in her confidence that death has lost its victory and sting and that one day she would rise victoriously with him. Doctrine does not divide, it unites; it does not harm, it heals. It reorients us in a disorienting world.

In the dark night of the soul, we may not need to learn more doctrine, but we need to be able to lean into the doctrine we already know. In the dark night of the soul, we do not need a lecture of divine providence, but we need to be able to lean into the beautiful truth and mystery of divine providence we already believe. Doctrine makes suffering tolerable because it reorients us to the Creator and his purposes in the world. As our people and churches experience darkness, they will lean into something. It will either be the glorious truths of who God is and what he has done in Christ, or it will be something else. They will trust something, so the church must give them something trustworthy. Christian belief is a stabilizing discipleship tool in a destabilizing and broken world. As my friend and colleague Kyle Worley says, "We shout doctrine in the light so that we can whisper it in the dark." When we do not disciple our people in basic Christian beliefs, we withhold the very thing they need to navigate our broken world.

Spiritual Habits

We are all formed by what we do. The habits we develop shape us into who we are. That is why the third core competency for holistic discipleship is helping our churches go deeper into fellowship with God through the practice of distinctly

Christian habits. We are not just minds that need to know doctrine but whole people who need to learn rhythms and habits that help us live into the story of God.

Distinctly Christian habits are precariously absent from most discipleship initiatives. Yet habits are inescapable—we all have them. Discipleship can tend to focus only on how what we *know* shapes us while simultaneously neglecting how what we *do* shapes us. As Justin Earley points out, "We are all living according to a specific regimen of habits, and those habits shape most of our life."[7]

We are formed by what we do, so one of the core competencies of growing disciples is learning how to practice Christian habits. Not only do we become what we worship, but we also become what we do.[8] The church has struggled to account for how powerful habits are in the life of disciples, and we have struggled to account for how habits that are not reflective of the gospel deform us. James K. A. Smith says, "Christian worship, . . . is essential *counter*formation to those rival liturgies we are often immersed in, cultural practices that covertly capture our loves and our longings, miscalibrating them, orienting us to

---

7. Justin Whitmel Earley, *The Common Rule: Habits of Purpose for an Age of Distraction* (Downers Grove, IL: IVP Books, 2019), 7.
8. G. K. Beale, *We Become What We Worship: A Biblical Theology of Idolatry* (Downers Grove, IL: Nottingham, England: IVP Academic, 2008).

rival versions of the good life."[9] The rhythms and habits of the world are forming our people, and the church that is focused on creating holistic disciples is offering counter rhythms and habits that form us into the people of God.

Churches that only focus on forming the mind will not be successful in shaping holistic disciples. The paradox of discipleship in the church is that we have so underestimated the power of formative habit that we have actually been formed more deeply by unintentional habits than we realize. The Bible's vision for holistic discipleship is for the whole person, not just a part of the person (Deut. 6:4–5; Luke 10:27). The church is called to invite disciples not only to love God with our whole selves but to be reminded that God loves our whole selves. That means no part of our lives is off limits; God wants all of us.

Churches, then, are to be places where disciples are called to integrate their minds with their hearts, their hearts with their souls, and their souls with their strength. Deep discipleship is aware of the whole person.

There are two ways churches should incorporate formative habits into a discipleship—corporate habits and individual habits. Corporate habits are the habits and rhythms the whole church is invited into. What the body does together shapes its individual members. The most obvious weekly habit the church participates in together is the gathering. Consistent

---

9. James K. A. Smith, *You Are What You Love: The Spiritual Power of Habit* (Grand Rapids, MI: Brazos Press, 2016), 25.

weekly attendance at the gathering is an essential characteristic of healthy churches. The local church is able to intentionally form people through formative worship services that have the whole person in view.

You are already shaping your people through the weekly gathering, but are you being as intentional as you could? Have you thought through how the order of service is forming your people? How intentional you are about the order of your weekly gathering matters because the weekly gathering is not just about informing minds but forming whole persons.

In the weekly gathering you have the opportunity to call the whole person to worship the one God, which is a reminder that all of the idols we were tempted to worship during the last week are indeed not God, because there is only one true God who is worthy of our worship. The church is able to corporately confess sin and lament over the brokenness of the world together. Through the preached Word, the whole person is, quite literally, able to sit under the Word and have the good news of the gospel proclaimed over them. I cannot emphasize enough how important it is to regularly participate in the ordinances of baptism and the Lord's Supper together as a body, as well as regular sacrificial giving. In these corporate habits the whole church is invited to live into the whole story as whole people.

Not only can the local church invite the whole people of God into corporate habits, but habit formation should be a part of your discipleship strategy for individuals. Which habits are appropriate for each person will depend on the discipleship space they are part of. The main point here is that you are never just teaching ideas but also always integrating those ideas into habits. People need to have space to do what they are growing to know.

For example, when the Training Program at The Village Church works through the doctrine of the providence of God, the students do not just read about providence and then hear a lecture on providence; they do a formation assignment on Sabbath that requires them to step away from the business of life and practice the sovereignty of God. It is not enough to read about the sovereignty of God; we also have to learn how to practice the sovereignty of God through habits. We invite our students to spend four hours with the Lord, practicing the sovereignty of God. Doctrine should be integrated into disciplines.

This is the work of integration. An integrated disciple loves God with her whole self, not just her mind. Whenever you are teaching part of the story of Scripture, or a part of Christian beliefs, those things must be integrated into spiritual habits that invite the whole person into discipleship. The story forms doctrine and doctrine forms our disciplines. Teaching void of habit formation tends toward Gnosticism. Habit formation void of teaching tends toward empty ritualism. Teaching and habit formation together tend toward wholeness—integration. Holistic disciples are integrating the true story of the world, the true beliefs contained in Scripture, and spiritual habits that form them into whole disciples.

Another example of habit formation occurs when we work through wisdom literature and the Psalms. Alongside teaching on these topics, we have students write out their own psalm or prayer to God. We encourage them to spend a few weeks writing, erasing, praying, and writing some more. This is a habit unfamiliar to most. They are used to extemporaneous prayers but not sustained, written prayer over the course of weeks. It is incredible to read their prayers and hear what they are asking God to do in their lives. It has made me a better pastor. After we collect the prayers, we incorporate them into a prayer book that we give to everyone who completes the Training Program. We also have incorporated those prayers into the corporate service so that our individual members are contributing to the collective gathering.

These three elements of the scope I am recommending are all integral to holistic discipleship. They are like a braid—if you leave any one of them out, the other two cease to hold together. They mutually inform and they are mutually interdependent.

What Disciples Need

Instead of asking the question, "What do disciples want?," we need to ask the better question, "What do disciples need?" The Bible, our beliefs, and our spiritual habits are what disciples need on the journey of going into deeper fellowship and communion with God in the local church. The Bible, beliefs, and habits are the foundation of a holistic scope of deep discipleship. These three are not nice discipleship outcomes but necessary discipleship outcomes. These core competencies represent the foundation of a scope of discipleship in the local church. The role of the local church is to invite people into participating in the true story of Scripture. The role of the local church is to instruct people in basic Christian beliefs. The role of the local church is to invite people into distinctly Christian formative habits that shape the whole person.

As the primary context for deep discipleship, local churches need to ask and answer the question not only of space—*Where are we forming people?*—but also of scope—*What do disciples need?* When we ask the important question of scope, we are able to guide and aim all of our ministry efforts toward equipping the saints with the competencies of deep discipleship. What do disciples need?

Main Ideas

1. The most effective churches realize that the sum of their ministries is greater than the parts. When each ministry has an understanding of how it contributes to the whole, we are able to do more together than apart.

2. Your scope represents what you think are the core competencies of discipleship—what you think is absolutely indispensable for your people to be learning and growing.

3. Instead of asking the question, "What do disciples want?," we need to ask the better question, "What do disciples need?"

Questions for Discussion

1. Do you agree that it is important for churches to determine an intentional scope of discipleship and build everything on that scope? Why or why not?

2. Discuss what you think are the indispensable elements of discipleship for which the local church is responsible. In other words, what are the nonnegotiables of discipleship?

3. What will happen to a church in the long run if it continues asking what disciples *want* rather than asking what they *need*?

To-Do List

1. Has your church been asking the question, "What do disciples want?" Or has it been asking the question, "What do disciples need?" What evidence is there for your answer? If you've been asking the first question, make a plan for shifting to the second.

2. Determine together a concise list of the indispensable elements of discipleship to which your church will be committed.

3. At the end of the last chapter, you categorized the list of ministries and programs currently active in your church. Now, as you come across each, ask: "How does this fit with the whole? Does it fall into any of the indispensable categories mentioned above?" If not, start thinking now about how you can transition out of that ministry or program, and discuss whether it should be replaced, and with what.

CHAPTER 5

Sequence: How Do Disciples Grow?

One of the most important things you can do is start raising the bar for your people. That sounds counterintuitive. We inherently think we need to put the cookies on the lowest shelf if people who are not yet mature disciples are going to have access. But the opposite is true. Disciples will never rise to an expectation the church does not set.

Knowing how to raise the bar, whom to raise the bar for, and when to raise the bar are essential elements of deep discipleship in the local church. The third question of deep discipleship in the local church, then, relates to sequence: How do disciples grow? How can the local church help holistic disciples take the next step in their spiritual growth and maturity? We have already looked at where disciples are formed (space) and advocated for the importance of dedicated and active learning environments in the local church. We also discussed what they need (scope) and encouraged the local church to make the important decision of training toward specific discipleship traits. Now it is time to give some attention to how deep disciples grow (sequence).

Usually churches are more accustomed to asking the question, "How do we maintain disciples in the local church?" Instead, we should ask the better question, "How do we grow disciples in the local church?" Sequence is all about creating progressively challenging discipleship spaces in the local church. These discipleship spaces function as a discipleship pipeline that encourages participants to take the next step of their development.

As you think about a sequence of discipleship in the local church, you are developing and implementing different stages of training that are appropriate to different maturity levels. The reason sequence matters is that it is important for the local church to guide believers into the deeper waters of the inexhaustible riches in God. The sequence of deep discipleship is motivated by the bottomless riches that are in Christ. Disciples take next steps not to graduate from a process but to enjoy more of God. In the local church we want our disciples to keep growing deeper into God because he alone is bottomless. You do not want maturing believers to have to stay in shallow waters when they are ready to go deeper, and you do not want to overwhelm baby believers in deeper waters when they need to slowly wade into deep discipleship. So, how can the local church guide believers into greater maturity, into increasingly deep discipleship over time?

Before we start talking about ways for the local church to help disciples grow, it is essential to remember that, biblically speaking, the Holy Spirit alone sanctifies and matures disciples. Salvation, from beginning to end, is the work of God. Sanctification cannot be sequenced by a program or a discipleship process. Writing to the Corinthians, Paul reminds them about their salvation by arguing: "And such were some of you. But you were washed, you were sanctified, you were justified in the name of the Lord Jesus Christ and by the Spirit of our God" (1 Cor. 6:11). Paul's Trinitarian picture of salvation is stunning and is meant to remind the Corinthians, and us, that God saves from beginning to end. Christians are washed by God, sanctified by God, and justified by God. Salvation is the work of the Father, through the Son, by the power of the Holy Spirit, from first to last.

It is good news that sanctification in the Christian life comes entirely through the empowering presence and ongoing ministry of the Holy Spirit in our lives. First Peter 1:2 argues that salvation is, "according to the foreknowledge of God the Father, in the sanctification of the Spirit, for obedience to Jesus Christ and for sprinkling with his blood." The Father initiates salvation. The Son accomplishes salvation. The Spirit applies salvation so that we may walk in obedience. In the Christian life there is no replacement for reliance on the Triune God. There is no path for deep discipleship other than living the Christian life by the power of the Holy Spirit; only he can make us whole again and conform us to the image of the Son. If not for the work of the Holy Spirit, all of our best ministry plans would be laid to nothing.

Yet another thread must be highlighted when it comes to the responsibility of the believer and the local church to grow in Christ. A constant theme in the New Testament is the call for disciples and for the local church to be active in their own spiritual growth. Paul called the Roman Christians to "present your bodies as a living sacrifice, holy and acceptable to God, which is your spiritual worship. Do not be conformed to this world, but be transformed by the renewal of your mind, that by testing you may discern what is the will of God, what is good and acceptable and perfect" (Rom. 12:1–2). The Christian life is one of increasing in maturity, as Paul encourages the Corinthians to "not be children in your thinking. Be infants in evil, but in your thinking be mature" (1 Cor. 14:20). Paul also tells the Philippian church that disciples are all straining toward the goal of Christ. He desired

> that by any means possible I may attain the resurrection from the dead. Not that I have already obtained this or am already perfect,

but I press on to make it my own, because Christ Jesus has made me his own. Brothers, I do not consider that I have made it my own. But one thing I do: forgetting what lies behind and straining forward to what lies ahead, I press on toward the goal for the prize of the upward call of God in Christ Jesus. Let those of us who are mature think this way, and if in anything you think otherwise, God will reveal that also to you. Only let us hold true to what we have attained. (Phil. 3:11–16)

The New Testament gives us the paradoxical picture that the Christian life is entirely of grace but that we are also called to grow in that grace. In other words, grace is not opposed to growth. Rather grace creates growth. Those who have received the grace of Christ also want to grow in Christ.

What is clear theologically is that God saves from beginning to end. Formation is entirely the work of the grace of God.[1] God's persevering grace is not weaker than his justifying grace. God's sanctifying work is not separated from his regenerating work. The gospel is not achieved by us; it is received by us. The gospel is not attained by merit; it is received by mercy.

---

1. Ellen T. Charry, *By the Renewing of Your Minds: The Pastoral Function of Christian Doctrine* (New York: Oxford University Press, 1999), 53.

But at the same time, Christians are called to strain forward, press on, and pursue maturity. Disciples train themselves for godliness (1 Tim. 4:7). The reception of the gospel creates a desire in disciples to grow in the gospel.

No amount of ministry effort and no amount of ministry excellence can bring about sanctification in the life of a believer—that is the responsibility of God and God alone. Do not overestimate the ability of your ministry strategy to grow people into the likeness of Christ. Yet the local church is also called to be a place that calls people to press on toward maturity, to take next steps in spiritual development, and to grow into Christ as whole disciples. A sequence of discipleship does not pretend to do the work of the Holy Spirit, but a sequence of discipleship also assumes that the Holy Spirit can use these spaces to grow mature disciples.

The gospel includes both justification and sanctification. That means our philosophy of ministry needs to be equally fueled by opportunities to respond to the gospel for the first time, for salvation, and for opportunities to go deeper and deeper into the gospel, for growth. We need to constantly remind people that the entirety of the Christian life is of grace, while at the same time calling them to grow in Christ. Dallas Willard helpfully points out: "Grace is not opposed to effort, it is opposed to earning. Earning is an attitude. Effort is an action."[2] This is so important for developing a holistic philosophy of ministry. A ministry philosophy that thinks effort is opposed to grace can never grow holistic disciples. In other words, just because sanctification is a work of the Spirit, that does not mean the church should not develop an intentional sequence of discipleship that the Holy Spirit may use to bring about increasing maturity among God's people.

God uses his church to grow people, which means we should think strategically about how a discipleship sequence can help believers in the church grow into maturity. If the local church is not calling people to press forward, to grow, to strain ahead, we will lose them. One of the paradigm shifts we need in ministry is the shift from asking the question, "How do we keep disciples in the church?" to the better question, "How do disciples grow in the church?" When we focus on keeping them, they remain immature, at best, and leave, at worst; when we focus on growing them, they mature. The first question shows that we are content to maintain disciples. The second question shows that we won't be content until we are making mature disciples.

---

2. Dallas Willard, *The Great Omission: Reclaiming Jesus's Essential Teachings on Discipleship*, Reprint ed. (New York: HarperOne, 2014), 61.

Don't Stunt Discipleship Growth

Sequence is ultimately the question of *how* we grow people by giving them increasingly challenging steps, information, or commitment. Sequence is intentional stages of training for your people, based on their growth and maturity. Your people should always know what next step, challenge, or opportunity is available to them. For example, we have already shown how the public school system has developed a scope—things like math, science, recreation, and social studies. These are the subjects they believe are important for developing responsible citizens. They have also developed a sequence of how to deliver that material over time in order to develop a growing student.

Take math, for example. Students start by learning how to count, then how to add and subtract, then how to multiply and divide, then how to do fractions, then geometry, then algebra, then trigonometry. This is an ongoing sequence of classes that calls them to mature as mathematicians. If the students were forced to start with algebra, they would never learn because they have not developed the basic mathematical competencies of addition and subtraction. If the students were left doing addition and subtraction, never pressing on to division and multiplication, they would never grow into students who can do geometry. The sequence of learning helps them take intentional next steps that are appropriate for their level of learning and maturity. When a student moves from addition and subtraction to multiplication and division, there is a sense of straining and pressing forward that is designed to help them grow. They are being asked to take the next step, to do something they do not know how to do, but it is not so large of a step that they will be unable to do it.

This principle is also true in fitness. One of my friends recently did a couch to 5K program that was designed to help her progressively adapt from not being able to run more than 400m without stopping to eventually running a 5K. If she started with a 5K, she likely would have given up in frustration, but if she just stayed on the couch, she never would have been able to do a 5K. Athletes who keep doing the same workout over and over will eventually plateau because their body is no longer being challenged. What they need is not more of the same but more repetitions, more weight, new exercises, etc. This is called adaptation—the body changes and grows based on new challenges and weight load.

This is a small picture of what sequence can look like in the local church. It is not enough to have learning spaces for discipleship in the local church. You also need to have active learning spaces that sequence discipleship outcomes for increasing maturity levels.

One of the reasons traditional models of Christian education have underperformed is that they failed to think strategically about how disciples grow. Most education-based models of discipleship, like Sunday school, are taught around an eighth-grade level of learning. This is perfect because that is where most people are starting in terms of their understanding of the Bible or other discipleship topics. But there is rarely a next-step or another space for people to transition to in order to challenge them.

For instance, I know a couple who have been in the same Sunday school class for almost forty years. Overall this class has been a wonderful discipleship space for them. It has helped them love Scripture and their community, and they are walking closer with Christ as a direct result of this class. However, they have never been challenged to take the next step past their Sunday school class. They have stayed at an eighth-grade discipleship level for the past forty years. They never were encouraged to strain forward to something more difficult or challenging. This discipleship model kept them, but it struggled to grow them. This would be the equivalent of a math student staying in an eighth-grade math class for forty years. If the local church is only discipling people at an eighth-grade reading level, we will only have eighth-grade-level disciples. There is absolutely nothing wrong with being at an eighth-grade maturity level if you are an eighth grader. It is only wrong when you are still in eighth grade but should be a teacher by now.

The author of Hebrews highlights the importance of sequence when he says: "For though by this time you ought to be teachers, you need someone to teach you again the basic principles of the oracles of God. You need milk, not solid food" (Heb. 5:12). He also later goes on to say, "Therefore let us leave the elementary doctrine of Christ and go on to maturity" (Heb. 6:1). One of the great tragedies in discipleship is being an infant when you should be an adult, a student when you should be a teacher. These passages are not suggesting that being a student, an infant, or drinking milk is a bad thing but that staying there is. Disciples eventually are meant to move from milk to meat (1 Cor. 3:2), from student to teacher, from child to adult. All of us are eventually called to leave the foundations of discipleship and press forward into being mature disciples of Christ—all through the power of the Holy Spirit—in the context of the local church.

The local church needs to have ways to progress people to the next step in their relationship with Christ—from student to teacher, from infant to adult, from milk to meat, just like the scenario I posed earlier about discipling your next pastor. We need to offer them discipleship spaces that do not leave them in the same place for forty years. We cannot be content with stagnant discipleship. We cannot stunt the growth of our people.

So, how can the local church develop next steps for a sequence of deep discipleship? A simple sequence of discipleship looks like this:

- A discipleship learning space that is for everybody
- A discipleship learning space that is for disciple-makers
- A discipleship learning space that is for disciple-making movements

These environments share more in common than you might think. They are all active learning environments, and they all share the same scope. Whatever scope of discipleship you decide on (Bible, beliefs, spiritual habits, etc.), you will teach it in all of these environments. You do not need to change what a disciple needs; you need to give them more of what they need but at a different level of maturity.

For example, in a discipleship space that is for everybody, you will be teaching Bible at an eighth-grade reading level, but in a discipleship space that is for disciple-makers, you will teach the Bible closer to a high school or undergrad reading level. Then in a discipleship space that is for your best leaders, you should be teaching it closer to a graduate level. What changes is the accessibility level you are training them at, not the type of content itself. The change occurs in the depth of the subject material, not the nature of the subject material. The primary feature that distinguishes these discipleship spaces is the level of accessibility. Each of these spaces is designed to allow everyone in the space to feel stretched.

Discipleship for Everybody

To go deep you have to start at the surface. The first part of your discipleship sequence should target everybody. It is essential that your church have a learning space in which everyone is welcome, including nonbelievers, new believers, and mature believers. These discipleship spaces are based on your scope of discipleship and designed to provide the kind of learning outcomes you want your entire church to have access to. Based on the scope I suggested in the last chapter, you should have learning spaces devoted specifically to helping people grow in Bible, theology, and spiritual formation. In these discipleship spaces you want to show that the Bible, theology, and spiritual formation are for everyone, not the spiritually elite.

If part of your scope is Bible literacy, then you want to offer a Bible study that is taught in such a way that every member can participate. I think the best way to do this is to offer a men's and women's Bible study that is open to everyone in the church and the community as well. Most people are intimidated by opening the Bible, so it is essential that the local church has learning spaces dedicated to helping people learn how to read Scripture.

I would also encourage you to make these environments multigenerational. I do not think you need to have an adult Bible study and a youth Bible study. You can separate those age groups in their small groups, which is appropriate, but it is so valuable for younger Christians to see adults continuing the learning process and for adults to see younger Christians take the first steps of the learning process. In these environments you have the opportunity to help Christians learn how to read Scripture for themselves.

If you have habit formation as part of your scope of discipleship, then you should have a learning space devoted specifically to helping your people learn how to participate in spiritual disciplines. Theology, church history, missions, apologetics—whatever your scope of discipleship is—offer a space for everyone to learn about what your church believes are the indispensable tools of discipleship in an accessible environment.

It is important to note that you are still raising the bar for people in this environment. These spaces are designed to be accessible to everyone but also stretching for everyone. Just because it is for everybody does not mean it should be easy. Remember, you want to create the right level of dissonance. You do not want it to be so easy that there is no reason for them to come, but you also do not want it to be so hard that they get discouraged.

You will find that these discipleship spaces also become great connection points for new people at your church. They provide a midsize environment that is not as large as your gathering but also not as small as a community group. Environments like that tend to be far less intimidating for people to enter as they seek to get involved in your church.

This is the part of the discipleship sequence where most churches stop. But what you are going to find is that if you start training your people in a conversational faith, they are going to want more. When you start training your people, you are going to see that they are not going to ask, "When are we done?" They are going to ask, "What is next?" Over time you are going to begin to see some people who are excelling in this space. They have been doing it for years, perhaps they have been leading a group for you, and they are asking for more. You need to have places where they can continue their journey of deep discipleship. The best discipleship spaces do not satisfy our desires; they shape our desires and create a hunger for more.

Discipleship for Disciple-Making Disciples

The second level of a discipleship sequence should move participants from consumption to contribution. In this space you are raising the bar higher than you raised it before. Here is where local churches have the opportunity to reclaim the church, not just as a domain of learning but as a substantive contributor to contemporary theology. You should establish prerequisites or requirements for participating in a discipleship space like this.

First, these participants should already be demonstrating a high level of commitment in the previous discipleship environment that is for everybody, because you are going to build on that foundation. Second, they need to be leading somewhere in your church. They may be leading a group of men or women in your Bible study, or they may be leading in your kids ministry, or they may serve on the parking team. It does not matter where they are leading, but you want to reserve this space for people who are demonstrating a deep desire to learn and who also are demonstrating a deep commitment to serving. The hope is that they will take what they learn in this environment to wherever they are serving in your church.

Again, one of the most important things you can do is to start to raise the bar for your people. It is impossible to create deep and holistic disciples if you are not raising the bar for them past an elementary learning space. In this discipleship space you are going to raise the bar past where you raised it before. This is where change and growth happen. This is where more dissonance happens. This is where your people will continue to grow as lifelong learners.

Remember, in this space you are not teaching new topics, but you are teaching at a deeper level. The scope of discipleship remains the same. You are still teaching Bible, theology, and spiritual formation, but you are inviting your students into deeper levels of participation in this space. You are going to see your students begin to move from consumption to contribution. They are going to become conversation partners with you, which shows that they are beginning to own the information for themselves.

Here are some examples of how to help your students move from consumption to contribution. If in your space that is designed for everyone you asked students to have a conversation about doctrine, in this space you are asking them to write doctrinal statements. If in your space that is designed for everyone you asked them to have a basic understanding of the story line of the Bible—like creation, fall, redemption, and consummation—in this space you are asking them to tell you the story of the Bible in twenty minutes. In this discipleship space you want them to make strides past where they ever thought they could go.

More people at your church are ready for a discipleship space like this than you know. I am continually surprised by the participants who turn out to be interested in this space. I thought my most eager and best participants would be young men who have been seminary trained or who are interested in going to seminary someday. I was expecting participants in this space to be considering ministry or missions and to be eager for more training for the vocation God is calling them into. While there have certainly been many great participants who fit that profile, that has not been the majority of people who have been interested and who have excelled in spaces like this. We have had tables full of men and women well into their seventies, and we have had more than a dozen high school students. We have had young families and empty nesters. You are going to find, if you start offering spaces like this, that people are desperate to grow. The way forward for deep discipleship is not lowering the bar; it is raising the bar. The most common feedback you will get from participants in these environments is, "I have been in the church my whole life, and nobody has told me this."

I also thought that spaces like this would be, at best, a 50/50 ratio between male and female. What I have found is that it is actually closer to a 60/40 female to male ratio. It made us realize that most discipleship spaces in the local church have an unintentional gender bias. First, this level of training has traditionally been outside of the local church, offered in a seminary or Bible college, which usually has more barriers for entry for women than it does for men. So when we opened this space, it was like offering water to a parched traveler. Discipleship that was previously only available outside the church was suddenly available for them in their local church, and they jumped on it.

Second, most community-driven discipleship spaces struggle to remove barriers for young families with kids, making it more challenging for moms to participate. We have seen young moms absolutely thrive in these spaces because they are finally invited into deeper discipleship in the context of their local church. This space also equips them with tools for discipling their kids. Churches need to realize that this level of training has historically not been accessible to them, and the cost of going to seminary is too high a price to pay. As we have reintroduced spaces like this in the local church, women have gravitated to spaces like this and have excelled.

For example, one student named Samantha had led a women's Bible study for years at our church and been involved in community groups. She was nervous about stepping into a more challenging environment but was also eager to learn.

Samantha is a mother of five kids and volunteers in a few ministries in the church. Suffice it so say, I shared her nervousness. I did not think she would be able to commit to a discipleship space like this. Given her life circumstances and how many other places she is serving in the church, I never thought she would have the desire to be in an intense discipleship program. I was wrong. Samantha completed the Training Program in its second year, came back as a table leader for the third year, and has served as our small-group director of the Training Program the past two years. She regularly says, "The Training Program changed my life, and I am never leaving." It is not because we were doing anything novel but because we were retrieving something recently forgotten—deep discipleship in the local church. Since then she has started several other ministries based on what she learned in the Training Program. She started a Public Reading of Scripture group that meets monthly to read entire books of the Bible out loud. She and a few other students also recently started a podcast to discuss what they are learning in the Training Program from a lay perspective. She moved from consumption to contribution.

Do not miss this: when you give people the tools for deep discipleship, they will begin discipling others. This is one of the best pictures of the priesthood of believers I have been able to be a part of, and it happened simply because we did not just want to keep people in the church but to grow them in the church.

In spaces like this we are showing everyone in the church that they have a seat at the table to do theology. Deep learning is not reserved for the elite but is available to everyone who is willing to take the step. More people are willing to take the step than you think, but you have to show them that doing theology is not as scary as they think it is.

An important feature in a discipleship space like this is the virtue of charity we already discussed. If a student asks the teacher a question that the teacher does not know, the teacher should say, "I do not know, but let's find out together." I cannot tell you how freeing it is for students to realize that even pastors and teachers are still on the journey of deep discipleship. These students will be empowered not just to learn but to make disciples, and the culture of discipleship at your church will be transformed.

Discipleship for Disciple-Making, Movement-Leading Disciples

One of the biggest misses is that our most committed disciples in the local church, those who want to lead churches and ministries, usually have to look outside the local church to learn how. Disciples should never have to leave the church in order to lead in the church. In this capstone space you are focused on making disciples who can lead the church or other kingdom-oriented organizations. These are your top-level leaders who have already excelled in your other discipleship spaces and have demonstrated a growing and increasing Christian maturity. This space is fairly exclusive because it is only available to people who have completed your previous learning environments, and it is by invitation only. Ultimately, this is where the local church is training elders, deacons, and other mature disciples.

When did it become acceptable to the church to have its best leaders trained outside of the church? Are you training your next group of elders, deacons, and other mature believers, or are they being formed outside the church? In residency-style programs the church has the opportunity to recover discipleship spaces for the men and women who are going to be the next generation of leaders in the local church.

A lot of churches have developed discipleship spaces like residencies for church planting or church revitalization, which I highly commend. Usually these discipleship spaces invite people from outside the church to apply to and move to the church for a season (usually a year or two) to be trained and sent out. Discipleship spaces like this are valuable and useful, but that is not what I am talking about.

The church's first responsibility is not to have environments that invite people from outside the local church to be trained but to train its own people. In other words, if your residency program is full of people who moved from another church and not people from your own church, I suggest there is a large gap in your discipleship sequence. It is possible that you are funding discipleship but not actually making disciples of your own members. Why are people from your church not filling up the residency program? If you are committed to the previous discipleship spaces, then you will have people who are prepared for this kind of discipleship sequence.

Our most intentional discipleship spaces in the local church, where we are committed to the highest level of investment and the highest level of excellence, should first be dedicated to the leaders in our church, not outside of it. If you are dependent on people applying from outside of your church for a residency program, I suggest investing in other discipleship spaces first until you have the kinds of participants in your church who are prepared for this kind of environment.

We have found it helpful to develop two tracks in our residency program: one track is dedicated to ministry leaders, the other to marketplace leaders. The discipleship culture of your church will never exceed the discipleship maturity of its leaders. If you do not have mature disciples, it is because you have not trained them. You need to have a discipleship space committed specifically to helping your future ministry leaders—elders and deacons—work toward biblical qualifications of those offices. We cannot rely on outside organizations to make leaders for the church; the church should own the primary weight of developing its own elders and deacons. Again, the scope of what you are giving to ministry leaders is still Bible, beliefs, and spiritual formation, but they are engaging at the level of what you would expect of a ministry leader. This is where you can develop preachers, teachers, shepherds, and servants who are growing in maturity.

I would also suggest having a parallel discipleship space for your marketplace leaders. One mistake that is often made is that the church thinks it is supposed to be in the business of leadership development. I understand this instinct, and leadership is certainly an important qualification for men and women you are leading in the marketplace. However, the primary function of the church is not to create leaders but disciples. In a marketplace residency you have the opportunity to invest in men and women who are already leading in the marketplace and help them to have a distinctly Christian impact in their sphere of influence. CEOs, teachers, doctors, and businessmen and women in your church want you to help them think through how the Bible, beliefs, and spiritual habits uniquely impact their vocation.

One of the goals in an environment like this is helping people move from reception to articulation. You are not just giving them information; they are contributing in meaningful ways to the conversation. You do not truly know something until you can articulate it. What if you had an environment that was dedicated to your most committed people, and you were investing so heavily in them that they became so familiar with Scripture, Christian beliefs, and spiritual habits that they naturally began helping others take steps of growth and maturity?

Deep discipleship culture is not dependent on a church staff; it is dependent on a well-trained congregation.

Churches should not just be asking the question, "How do we keep disciples?" We should be asking the better question, "How do we grow disciples?" Philosophies of ministry that only have the highest stated value of community are focused on keeping disciples. Philosophies of ministry that have the highest stated value of learning, like Sunday school, but do not have a sequence of discipleship are also too focused on keeping disciples. But if we implement a philosophy of ministry that values learning environments, in the context of community, and also allow disciples to take next steps through a sequence of learning, we will make maturing disciples of Christ.

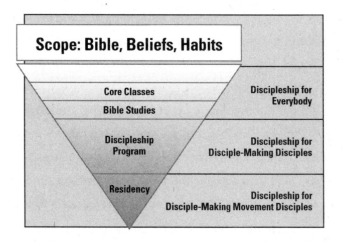

Scope: Bible, Beliefs, Habits

Core Classes	Discipleship for
Bible Studies	Everybody
Discipleship Program	Discipleship for Disciple-Making Disciples
Residency	Discipleship for Disciple-Making Movement Disciples

Main Ideas

1. Knowing how to raise the bar, whom to raise the bar for, and when to raise the bar are essential elements of deep discipleship in the local church.

2. You do not want maturing believers to have to stay in shallow waters when they are ready to go deeper, and you do not want to overwhelm baby believers in deeper waters when they need to slowly wade into deep discipleship.

3. If the local church is not calling people to press forward, to grow, to strain ahead, we will lose them. One of the paradigm shifts we need in ministry is the shift from asking the question, "How do we keep disciples in the church?," to the better question, "How do disciples grow in the church?"

Questions for Discussion

1. Are you naturally wired to think the Holy Spirit will use a sequence of discipleship to sanctify Christians or to think a sequence will be a hindrance to the Holy Spirit's work? What personality traits or past experiences have wired you this way?

2. Why is it important to remember that when you move deeper into discipleship, you're not moving on to different content, but moving into the same content—namely, God and his gospel?

3. Is your church currently providing opportunities for people to go deeper in discipleship, or has it been too focused on merely maintaining members?

To-Do List

1. Now that you listed your essential discipleship categories (scope) in the last chapter, start brainstorming what different levels (sequence) of each category might look like. What needs to be offered in each category for the skeptic, the new believer, the child, the teenager, the seventy-year-old saint, the seminary graduate?

2. Develop a plan for communicating to your congregation this intentional move of developing a discipleship sequence. How can you explain to them that the Holy Spirit will use an intentional structure to sanctify people? How can you communicate the notion of a discipleship sequence without appearing to create a discipleship hierarchy?

3. Pray together that God would bless your attempts to create an intentional scope and sequence of discipleship in the local church. Ask the Spirit to use your efforts to sanctify his people. Ask God if there's anything you're missing, if there are any adjustments you need to make to the rough draft of a scope and sequence you've created.

CHAPTER 6

Send: Where Do Disciples Go?

A few years ago a young woman named Hope participated in our Training Program. She was a nurse at a local hospital, and she was a longtime faithful member of our church. She had never really considered world missions as a part of what God might be calling her into but was faithfully participating in the mission of God in her spheres of influence.

She was in a discipleship space that taught through the Gospel of Matthew over a weekend. It was nothing fancy—just an introduction to Gospel literature, hermeneutics, and a basic overview and exposition of the text. Yet, through a basic reading of Matthew, Hope began to better understand the story of Scripture, who Jesus was, and what it means to be a disciple. Specifically, she was captivated by a richer meaning of the Great Commission at the end of the Gospel. This was not a seminar on world missions but a seminar on how the Gospels form us as disciples. It was not a seminar on why we should go to unreached people groups. It was not a seminar on church planting. It was just a simple seminar on the Gospel of Matthew. But through this seminar the mission of God got into her blood.

Churches are used to asking the question, "Where do *some* disciples go?" But we should ask the better question, "Where do *all* disciples go?" We cannot just focus on sending missionaries and church planters—though we can never stop planting churches and missionaries. But a culture of deep discipleship is intent not on sending a few but on sending all.

I know that some churches have a concern that if they focus too intently on discipleship, they may not be as focused on mission. I heard one pastor say that a church that focuses on discipleship feasts on the Bible but fasts from mission.

This couldn't be further from the truth.

It is another example of the either/or mentality. *Either* we will be a church that focuses on discipleship, *or* we will be a church that focuses on mission. It's certainly possible that some churches who focus on discipleship neglect mission, but to do so reveals that their "discipleship" focus isn't truly a focus on discipleship at all. Discipleship is about being a learner of Jesus, and the mission of Jesus was to seek and save the lost. He commanded us to take the gospel to all peoples. If our disciple-ship doesn't lead to mission, we're not producing disciples of Jesus.

A deep discipleship church, therefore, is also a missional church. A church that trains is also a church that sends. Christian maturity does not hinder mission; it fuels mission. The multiplication of churches starts with the multiplication of mature disciples.

Holistic disciples love God with all their heart and with all their soul and with all their strength and with all their mind, and they also love their neighbor as themselves (Luke 10:27; Matt. 22:37–40). Jesus gives us this picture of holistic disciple-ship, the Great Commandment, as a means by which to recen-ter our whole selves on God. He also instructs his followers to make more people who love God as they do. After his resurrec-tion Jesus instructed his disciples: "All authority in heaven and on earth has been given to me. Go therefore and make disciples of all nations, baptizing them in the name of the Father and of the Son and of the Holy Spirit, teaching them to observe all that I have commanded you. And behold, I am with you always, to the end of the age" (Matt. 28:18–20). The picture the Gospels give us is that Great Commandment Christians are called to replicate themselves in the Great Commission.

The Great Commission will be fulfilled by Great Commandment Christians. To be a Great Commandment Christian is to love God with your whole self and to love your neighbor. The Great Commission is to create Great Commandment Christians. The Great Commandment invites us to participate in the Great Commission, and the Great Commission invites us to participate in the Great Commandment.

If we abandon the Great Commandment, we will undermine the Great Commission. The mission of Jesus is not to create half-hearted disciples but whole disciples, people who love God with their whole self and their neighbor as themselves. There is no tension between the Great Commandment and the Great Commission but rather synergy. Training and mission are meant to fuel each other. If you start by going deep, you will also be forced to go wide. If you start by going wide, you will never go deep.

Where Do Disciples Go?

We have discussed space: where disciples are formed; scope: what disciples need; and sequence: how disciples grow. An equally important question for deep discipleship is about sending: Where do disciples go? A central element of a church that is pursuing deep discipleship is intentionally commissioning disciples to participate in the mission of God. It is not enough to form deep disciples; we have to be equally intentional about sending deep disciples. For deep discipleship to take root in your church, you need to be equally focused on training and sending. A church that focuses on training without sending is missionless. A church that focuses on sending without training is purposeless.

In every discipleship space you should ask your participants, "What are you learning, and whom are you teaching what you are learning?" Discipleship never terminates on itself, but all disciples go and make other disciples. To be a disciple of Jesus is to make other disciples of Jesus. Multiplication is baked into the definition of what it means to be a disciple. The reason the local church forms deep disciples is so they can experience deeper communion with God and also participate in his mission of inviting others into fellowship with Christ. There is no such thing as a disciple of Christ who is not making other disciples of Christ. Disciples make disciples. The local church has an opportunity to both train and send, to equip people and commission people. Send everyone you train and train everyone you send.

But it is not enough to be committed to the idea of sending people. It is important that you have intentional pathways for sending and commissioning people to participate in the mission of God. Churches that are pursuing a culture of deep discipleship are intentionally commissioning their disciples into the church, the home, their neighborhoods, the workplace, and the nations.

The Church

Being sent is not for the spiritually elite; it is for every Christian. One of the most overlooked aspects of sending is intentionally sending disciples back into the local church to serve and lead. I know that it sounds a little counterintuitive to think of the local church as the first place to intentionally send people, but I also think it is deeply biblical. Ephesians 4:12 reminds us that one of the primary purposes of discipleship in the local church is to build more disciples who build up the body of Christ. Every believer is called to ministry and service in the local church. One of the clearest ideas the New Testament gives us is that we are all called to build up the body of Christ through service. When the church becomes a place where people are an audience, rather than participants, we have moved far away from the New Testament's understanding of discipleship. Ministry is not something the church staff does; it is something the whole church does. The responsibility of the local church is not to put on a show but to call and equip others into service.

Christ has given foundational gifts to the church—apostles, prophets, evangelists, shepherds, and teachers—in order to equip all the saints to do ministry. Too often the church can act as if the foundational gifts of apostle, prophet, evangelist, shepherd, and teacher are the only gifts because those are the ones that get all the attention. The church is not meant to put the talented on a stage but the gifted into service, and all are gifted. Each believer functions with spiritual gifts that are meant to be put into the service of the church, in order to build up the body of Christ. The role of the church staff is not to do ministry for people but to equip all people to do ministry.

Romans 12 paints a similar picture:

> For as in one body we have many members, and the members do not all have the same function, so we, though many, are one body in Christ, and individually members one of another. Having gifts that differ according to the grace given to us, let us use them: if prophecy, in proportion to our faith; if service, in our serving; the one who teaches, in his teaching; the one who exhorts, in his exhortation; the one who contributes, in generosity; the one who leads, with zeal; the one who does acts of mercy, with cheerfulness. (vv. 4–8)

Paul is saying that all the members of the body of Christ are dependent on serving one another. We need one another. When the local church does not have simple pathways and trajectories for people to be commissioned back into the local church to serve and to lead, we communicate to them that we do not need them. Each person in your church has been given a gift to serve the body, to contribute to the good of the whole.[1]

---

1. Leon Morris, *The Epistle to the Romans* (Grand Rapids: Eerdmans, 1988), 438.

When you send and empower them to serve in the church, everyone is better for it, and you communicate the gospel truth that we are one body and many members, each in need of the others.

Serving and leading in the local church in meaningful ways is the incubator for mission. In comparison to sending disciples to the ends of the earth, this can feel a bit self-serving for a church. It can feel like we are more interested in our own needs and not the needs of others. I understand that impulse, but commissioning disciples into service in the local church is actually what enables the commissioning of people to the ends of the earth. Most people you disciple will not be sent abroad, but they can contribute meaningfully to a healthy local church. As they contribute to a healthy local church discipleship culture, they will enable and fuel others to go make disciples among the nations. If we are not making disciples in the church, we will never make disciples among the nations.

There are two places to send and commission people into the life of the local church. First, you can send disciples back into the discipleship spaces they have already participated in. When you think about the discipleship sequence you create for your church, whatever space comes before the environment a disciple is in, they should be able to lead, or at least facilitate, in that environment. For example, someone who has graduated from a residency environment should be able to lead a small group in a previous teaching environment. Some of them will even be able to teach in an environment like a men's or women's Bible study. Your discipleship program graduates should be your best leaders in your men's and women's Bible studies. Many of these environments will be life-changing for these men and women, so the opportunity to serve in these environments will be massive for them. They will have the opportunity to see the same deep discipleship in others they have experienced for themselves. You will also see that, as they become teachers and facilitators themselves, they will learn the material better than they ever have before.

One instinct you will have to avoid as you set up all of these spaces dedicated to learning is the instinct to staff everything out to paid ministers. Once you have equipped others, you have to send them to equip others as well. Show them that their equipping matters, that once they are equipped they are going to be able to use the new tools they have in order to serve and lead others. There are certainly some things that should be handled by elders and pastoral staff, but a lot of these learning spaces should be led, taught, and facilitated by members of your church. Rather than staffing all discipleship spaces, send people into those spaces whom you have already trained, and give them the responsibility of equipping others. A huge opportunity for you is to invite people to be participants in these discipleship spaces, not audience members. You will find that the deepest discipleship happens when they are able to own parts of the discipleship sequence.

Second, not only should you send people back into a learning space, but you can send disciples back into other ministries in the local church. During the first year of the Training Program at The Village Church Institute, I was worried that asking for such a big commitment from people might mean that they would stop serving in other ministries in the church. I even had several staff express concern that they were going to lose many of their volunteers. I thought that our student ministry volunteers or our group leaders might take a year off in order to participate in the one-year Training Program. Maybe the team that serves in our recovery ministry would not be able to continue leading while they were in the Training Program. In light of that concern, we decided to make serving in another ministry while you were completing the Training Program a requirement for admission. We decided not to accept anyone into the Training Program who was not serving elsewhere in the church. We were committed to this principle because we want to provide the best training and equipping for the people who are already serving the church, not just people who wanted to take a class. This principle proved to be invaluable because not only did it improve the applicant pool, but it provided them an outlet to share and teach others what they were learning.

Something we began noticing almost immediately was how the culture of the Training Program was making its way into other discipleship ministries in the church. Home group leaders began taking their home groups through similar curriculum. A group of guys who were leading a high school Bible study began taking their students through the basics of Christian doctrine. Our leaders in the preschool and elementary school ministries began revising some of their curriculum to match more closely what they were being trained in.

One of my favorite things at church over the past few years has been taking my two kids, Thomas and Bailey, to their preschool ministry classrooms during worship service. These leaders in our family ministries are some of the most dedicated and devoted disciple-makers in the church. One classroom in particular was led by a couple who were going through the Training Program that year. He was working as an oil executive, and she was busy serving in various ministries in the church. When they entered the Training Program, I was worried that they were not going to be able to maintain all of their commitments, especially serving in our kids ministry. What I realized over the course of the year was that not only were they able to maintain their commitments, but they actually became more committed to them.

They experienced a renewed fuel and fire to what they were doing. I would walk by their classroom and hear how they were teaching and explaining the Bible with a renewed vigor. They were using language similar to that they were hearing in the Training Program but making it accessible for preschoolers. They led our three-year-old room at church, and when I dropped my kids off there, almost every week the curriculum they were working through, the prayers they were learning, and the stories they were hearing were directly related to what they had learned the week before in the Training Program. I began to hear my son use language from the Training Program that he was hearing not from me but from our participants. They have responded to the question, "What are you learning, and whom are you teaching it to?" by taking what they have learned in the Training Program and teaching it in the kids ministry. Deep discipleship is most clear when the people you are training are sent to train others.

This couple is living proof that deep discipleship doesn't distract from mission; it fuels it. They described their experience as being both trained and intentionally sent as no longer being volunteers in the preschool ministry but as leaders in the preschool ministry. Their work was not nice but necessary. Their service was infused with more meaning now because they could see how the investment we were making in them was also making its way to others. They began to see themselves rightly not just as recipients of a discipleship curriculum but as conduits of a discipleship lifestyle. They realized that they were not just volunteers but indispensable ministry partners in the church.

One of the biggest opportunities for the local church, when you train and send people to serve in your own local church, is to create a shared discipleship culture across all ministries. One of the biggest threats to a church that wants to pursue deep discipleship is ministry silos. If you only have a culture of deep discipleship in one of your ministries, it will never work. All ministries need to share this vision of deep discipleship, and this is made possible when ministries are intentionally equipping their people to go serve in other ministries.

What if the scope and sequence you create could be shared by all ages? Then, when you are training people in Bible studies, a training program, core classes, or a residency, you are equipping them with the categories and language they can use in spaces you are commissioning them into. If you are training people intentionally around the story of the Bible, basic Christian beliefs, and spiritual habits, they will be able to use and appropriate that language in any ministry they are serving. This is what we saw with this couple and so many other leaders—they were able to take the language and ideas we were using in our discipleship learning spaces and use it in appropriate ways as they served kids.

People don't graduate from discipleship; they are commissioned into further discipleship. It is important that you begin using language like this. When people finish your Bible study, core class, training program, or a residency, they do not graduate; they are commissioned. There are no graduates from learning spaces, only commissioned participants. It's important for your people to realize that, as they participate in your discipleship sequence, they are not completing a course that they graduate from but a course that commissions them back into the life of the church to serve.

One year we decided to rewrite our Vacation Bible School curriculum. Our preschool staff asked some of our members to help with the writing process. All of these members were graduates of the Training Program, and since they had been commissioned back into serving the church, they were prepared for this responsibility. They took everything they learned in the Training Program and simplified it into a curriculum that was age appropriate. They built out worksheets, videos, and songs all based on the things they had been equipped in and commissioned to give to others. This was discipleship that was not handed over to the staff but completely done by men and women who had been trained and deployed to serve the church.

Think about how momentous this could be for your church. When you intentionally disciple your leaders and create intentional pathways for leading in your church, you will be stunned by the results. I was always a little concerned that the quality of discipleship would suffer if we released church members to do it, but I could not have been more wrong. The quality actually got better. This meant that not only were we discipling a few hundred people in the Training Program, but our participants were taking what they were learning and teaching it to hundreds of others in our church. This is the best of what training and sending into the local church can look like. When we value both training and sending, we democratize discipleship in the local church.

When you intentionally train people in the local church and commission them back into the local church, you are not neglecting the Great Commission; you are helping to fulfill it. Your members *are* the local church, so they are meant to impact it, not just be impacted by it. Not only church staff members participate in the mission of God; every member is a participant. Empower your people to participate in the mission of God in the local church by not only training them but also intentionally sending them to serve and to lead. Train everyone you send and send everyone you train.

Homes and Neighborhoods

Not only are disciples sent into the local church, but they are also commissioned back into their homes and neighborhoods. Spouses, parents, grandparents, and singles should all be commissioned back into their homes and neighborhoods to make disciples.

Some of the healthiest spiritual fruit we have seen coming out of our learning spaces is spouses growing deeper in the Lord together. The men's and women's Bible studies, though they meet separately, cover the same books of the Bible and use the same curriculum. This has created wonderful conversations for our married couples that have allowed them to see their home as a place for spiritual development in new ways. The husbands are able to share what they are learning with their wives, and wives are able to share with their husbands what God is teaching them.

A lot of churches talk about it being the parents' responsibility to disciples their kids, and they are right, but that only works if you are intentionally training the parents in the church and empowering them to spiritually form their children in the home. When moms and dads take the gospel to their homes and disciple their kids, they are obeying the Great Commission. A mom does not have to go overseas to participate in the Great Commission; she can also go to the nursery. A dad does not have to go overseas to participate in the Great Commission; he can drive his children to school and back. It is one thing to see the home as a place for spiritual development; it is another thing to equip parents to make their home a place for discipleship. One of the best things we can do for the spiritual development of the next generation is for them to see older generations walking closely with the Lord. The home is the primary place for them to see what deep discipleship looks like from their parents.

The fastest way to take the gospel to the nations is to take it to our neighbors. Of course the local church should be taking the gospel to the ends of the earth, but before we take the gospel to the ends of the earth, we should take it to the end of the street. The people we eventually send to the nations are the people who are already sent to their neighbors. We should not send anybody to make disciples of the nations who is not already making disciples of their neighbors.

Churches with a culture of deep discipleship should celebrate the missional movement of the last decade. At their best, missional churches plant churches, transform communities, and reach people with the good news of Christ. However, one thing we have learned about the missional movement is the danger of sending people before forming people. We have made the mistake of sending people who have not yet been formed themselves.

Mission without formation is suicide for a church.

If we send people who have not been deeply discipled in the local church, they will be discipled more by who we send them to. Missionally minded churches that are helping their people see their neighbors as a mission field must be equally committed to forming their people for the mission. It takes a disciple to make a disciple.

That is why it is so important for the church to form people and then send them back into their communities. The Great Commission does not start with going to the nations but to their neighbors.

Workplace

In the garden God gave humanity not only his presence but a purposeful existence: work. "The LORD God took the man and put him in the garden of Eden to work it and keep it" (Gen. 2:15). In the Christian worldview work is inherently good. Certainly sin taints humanity's relationship to its labors (Gen. 3:17–19), but God's primary intention is to give humanity purpose in work as humans cultivate God's creation. It is not an exaggeration to say that humanity's primary commission is to work, cultivate, and care for God's creation.[2] Even while Israel was in exile in Babylon, they were reminded by the prophet Jeremiah of their calling to cultivate, steward, and care for God's creation:

> Thus says the LORD of hosts, the God of Israel, to all the exiles whom I have sent into exile from Jerusalem to Babylon: Build houses and live in them; plant gardens and eat their produce. Take wives and have sons and daughters; take wives for your sons, and give your daughters in marriage, that they may bear sons and daughters; multiply there, and do not decrease. But seek the welfare of the city where I have sent you into exile, and pray to

---

2. Kenneth Mathews, *The New American Commentary: Genesis 1–11:26* (Nashville: Holman Reference, 1996), 209.

the LORD on its behalf, for in its welfare you
will find your welfare. (Jer. 29:4–7)

Work is God's idea, and all of us are given the responsibility to
work for the good of those around us.

Many of the men and women we minister to either have a
hard time seeing their work as good, or they see their work as
the ultimate good. Either they believe their work is not worth
doing, or they believe it is the only thing worth doing. Either
work is purposeless, or it is their only purpose. When the local
church trains and sends its members into the workplace, we
have the opportunity to show them that when the mission of
God frames our work, no work is purposeless, and no work is
our primary purpose.

The primary work of Christians in the marketplace is mission. All Christians are ministers; the only thing that changes
is context. "By our work, the naked are clothed, the hungry
are fed, and the sick are healed. By our labor we love our
neighbors. Toiling in our God-given place, we become God's
agents."[3] Local churches have the opportunity to recast and
reenvision for Christians how their work is infused with meaning and opportunity for gospel ministry.

As I was writing this, I received a text in a group thread
from one of our former Marketplace Residency participants.

---

3. Daniel M. Doriani, *Work: Its Purpose, Dignity, and Transformation*
(Phillipsburg, NJ: P&R Publishing, 2019), 66.

She works in the marketing industry at a major firm in Dallas, and for the longest time she struggled to see her vocation as an opportunity for discipleship. She considered changing her career to full-time vocational ministry and even started to go to seminary part-time. In her text she shared with the group about all of the conversations she is having with her coworkers about the story of Scripture. She said that most of them did not know the Bible is a unified story; they believed it was just a book of morals, rules, and commands. She was able to share the story of Scripture with them, from the perspective of work, and her coworkers were amazed that the theme of work could be traced through the Bible from beginning to end. This conversation, she commented, helped her see that her work is meaningful and that God can use her in her vocation for his kingdom.

One of the greatest benefits to come out of the Protestant Reformation was the recovery of a Christian understanding of work. The priesthood of believers certainly applies to a ministry context: all Christians are ministers of reconciliation and have gifts to build up the church. But we also need to be reminded that the priesthood of believers applies to a marketplace context: all work done for the glory of God brings glory to God. When we commission our people into their vocations, they are reminded that what they do matters to God, that there is not a sacred-secular divide when it comes to vocation, and that all meaningful work brings glory to God.

Yet, in the church today, many Christians still believe that vocational ministry is more meaningful than working in the marketplace, education, or medical fields. One of the most important things you can do for your people is to remind them of the importance of their work, to reinfuse gospel meaning into their everyday lives. Churches that are committed to deep discipleship want their best disciple-makers to be commissioned into their vocations as men and women whose work is infused with the purpose of the kingdom of God.

The Nations

Finally, a church that is passionate about forming deep disciples in the church is also passionate about forming deep disciples among the nations. Churches that are committed to deep discipleship are also committed to missions and church planting among the unreached. We should want to send our most trained, mature, and godly men and women to start gospel movements among the nations. One of the primary missions of the local church is to plant more healthy local churches across the globe. But we cannot plant healthy, multiplying churches among the unreached until we have healthy, multiplying disciples among ourselves.

We have learned two lessons about sending missionaries and church planters to the field. The first lesson is that we cannot expect missionaries to become deep and holistic disciples on the field if they are not deep and holistic missionaries before they go to the field. We cannot expect missionaries to do on the field what they are not doing at home. Local churches can have a tendency to send missionaries to the field expecting them to become healthy Christians while there, but this is a misguided instinct that compromises our ability to plant churches and reach the lost. Missionaries and church planters go into some of the most emotionally, relationally, physically, and spiritually disorienting environments in the world. If they are not shaped in the Bible, Christian beliefs, and spiritual habits before they go, they will not have any gauges to reorient them.[4]

The second lesson we learned was the importance of the local church in sending missionaries to the unreached. The most qualified and effective church planters and missionaries are trained in the local church. I am grateful for all sending agencies around the globe, but sending agencies are most effective when they work closely with the local church. Too often the local church abdicates its responsibility of sending missionaries to mission agencies, believing the mission agency is more equipped to train and send missionaries. Missions organizations are able to provide specialized training, such as language skills and contextualization, but there is no substitute for the local church in sending disciples to fulfill the Great Commission. As the local church reengages in the task of creating learning spaces in the local church, we are also going to

---

4. See chapter 4.

have the opportunity to send our most mature and Christlike disciples to the ends of the earth.

There is no dichotomy between training and sending or equipping and commissioning. Train every person in your church and send every person in your church—that is deep and holistic discipleship. Equip every person in your church and deploy every person in your church. Holistic formation is not a hindrance to mission, and mission is not a limitation to holistic formation. Instead, deep discipleship and mission, training, and sending, are meant to work together and complement one another. Deep discipleship is the fuel for mission.

The Great Commission is going to be fulfilled in our churches, our homes, our neighborhoods, our workplaces, and ultimately the nations, and it is going to be fulfilled by deep disciples who are committed to the glory of God above all else.

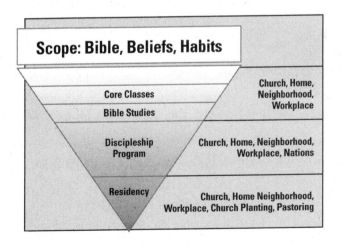

Main Ideas

1. A culture of deep discipleship is not intent on sending a few, but on sending all. A deep discipleship church is also a missional church. A church that trains also sends. Christian maturity does not hinder mission; it fuels mission. The Great Commission will be fulfilled by Great Commandment Christians.

2. A central element of a church that is pursuing deep discipleship is intentionally commissioning disciples to participate in the mission of God. It is not enough to form deep disciples; we have to be equally intentional about sending deep disciples.

3. Churches that are pursuing a culture of deep discipleship are intentionally commissioning their disciples into the church, the home, their neighborhoods, the workplace, and the nations.

Questions for Discussion

1. Have you heard people express the notion that discipleship and mission somehow compete with each other in the local church? Why is that thinking misguided and unbiblical?

2. Have you ever been a part of a local church with a commissioning culture? If so, what did that look like? If not, what might it look like if your church developed this culture?

3. Why is it not only preferable but essential for disciples to be commissioned into service as they are growing? In other words, why is it essential for them to pour out while they're being filled up?

To-Do List

1. Discuss together some of the dangers inherent in a so-called "discipleship" culture that is not intent on sending all of its members into ministry.

2. Does your church currently have a commissioning culture? If so, what does that look like practically? If not, how can you adopt this?

3. Take a look at your working scope and sequence. Discuss what it would look like to send disciples into the church, the home, their neighborhoods, the workplace, and the nations, from your discipleship spaces.

CHAPTER 7

Strategy: Adopting a Holistic Approach to Discipleship

As we come to the close of this book, we have already thought through several important questions about creating a culture of deep discipleship in the local church. First, we spent some time thinking about the question of space: Where are disciples formed? Every church needs to think through the intentional spaces they are creating in order for discipleship to take place. Specifically, I argued that one of the key elements of local churches making disciples is the retrieval of learning environments. I argued that not only is it important for churches to retrieve learning environments but also that they must be transformational and active learning environments, environments where disciples are invited into meaningful community where the highest stated goal is learning.

Second, we dealt with the question of scope: What do disciples need? Too many churches have not answered the essential questions around the learning outcomes and competencies related to discipleship. I argued that it is essential for local churches to think carefully about the key learning outcomes and competencies they want to see in their disciples. At a basic level, I advocated that local churches should be training their disciples in the Bible, basic Christian beliefs, and spiritual formation/habits.

Third, we considered the question of sequence: How do disciples grow? I argued that the local church should intentionally create sequenced discipleship environments, specifically designed to challenge and grow mature disciples of Christ. Too many of our spaces in the local church allow for stagnation, but if we create environments designed to encourage next steps and growth, we will see disciples grow in their maturity over time.

Fourth, we looked at the question of sending: Where do disciples go? I argued that there is not a dichotomy between a church that trains and a church that sends. A church that is passionate about discipleship is also a church that is passionate about mission. Churches that grow deep also grow wide. A key element here is that we should always be asking our disciples, "What are you learning, and who are you teaching it to?" All disciples are invited into the disciple-making process and are given intentional pathways into serving in the local church, their homes and neighborhoods, the workplace, and ultimately the nations. Churches that are focused on making holistic disciples train and send everybody.

It's time to turn our attention to the final question. Instead of asking, "Can my church do this?," I want you to ask the better question, "Why would my church *not* do this?"

Until this point, we have thought through some important ideas for your ministry context, but none of it matters unless your church has the desire and the ability to execute this vision. I want to make the case that the vision of deep discipleship we have covered so far is scalable to any church, sustainable in any church, and strategic for any church.

Some of the most frequent questions I am asked when I talk to church leaders about deep discipleship relate to scalability: Can my church do this? I understand this question because some of this can feel overwhelming. Ministry is incredibly challenging. It can feel like there is always another fire to put out, another message to prepare, or another meeting to attend. I have asked myself this question before because it is easy to think that everything we have covered so far can only be implemented at a church with enormous resources, a large congregation, and a huge ministry staff. Is this a megachurch approach to discipleship, or can it be implemented in every kind of church? It is easy to believe that only churches with a large staff, a large building, and a bought-in congregation will be able to adequately develop discipleship spaces, scope, sequence, and intentional sending. But is it possible for this vision of discipleship to be implemented by a church of fewer than a thousand? How about a church of fewer than five hundred? What about a church smaller than one hundred people? Does this require dozens of staff members, or can this be done by a ministry staff of four or five people? Can a bivocational pastor implement the philosophy of ministry outlined in this book? To all of these questions I want to answer an emphatic yes!

Deep discipleship does not require massive resources, a large congregation, or an enormous ministry staff. In fact, I would say that one of the most attractive aspects of deep discipleship is that it is scalable to any church context. Too many ministry philosophies are applicable only to a certain kind of ministry setting or a certain type of church. That is not the case with deep discipleship. Deep and holistic discipleship is ultimately about asking and answering each of these questions in a way that is consistent with where you are:

> Space: Where does discipleship happen in the church?
>
> Scope: What do disciples need?
>
> Sequence: How do disciples grow?
>
> Send: Where do disciples go?

These essential questions apply to any and every ministry context, and the answers are scalable to whatever context you are applying them.

Was Jesus' Ministry Scalable?

I think we even see the question of ministry scalability in Christ's earthly ministry. In other words, Jesus intentionally scaled his ministry for his context. In Jesus' ministry we can see intentional spaces for discipleship, a purposeful scope of discipleship, a focused sequence of discipleship, and an intentional sending of the disciples.

Jesus employed various spaces in his discipleship ministry. The Bible depicts Jesus teaching in synagogues, on hillsides, in homes, and to individuals. He was intentionally using various spaces in order to teach and equip the men and women who were following him.

Jesus also had a specific discipleship scope in his ministry. The Gospels show that the content of Jesus' teaching was primarily the gospel of the kingdom. He never strayed from the message of the kingdom. He approached it from different angles; he used parables, stories, and imagery familiar to his audience, but the scope of what he taught never changed.

I believe Jesus also had some kind of discipleship sequence that helped his disciples grow. The Gospels depict him ministering to crowds, to large groups of followers, to the twelve disciples, and to the three disciples. He does not neglect the few for the crowd, and he does not neglect the crowd for the few. Jesus did not invest in the crowds the same way he invested in his closest disciples. With both time and content he was making different investments with various groups.

For example, we see Jesus minister to large crowds in Matthew 4:23–25:

> And he went throughout all Galilee, teaching in their synagogues and proclaiming the gospel of the kingdom and healing every disease and every affliction among the people. So his fame spread throughout all Syria, and they brought him all the sick, those afflicted with various diseases and pains, those oppressed by demons, those having seizures, and paralytics, and he healed them. And great crowds followed him from Galilee and the Decapolis, and from Jerusalem and Judea, and from beyond the Jordan.

This text is immediately followed by Jesus teaching a large crowd in the Sermon on the Mount. "Seeing the crowds, he went up on the mountain, and when he sat down, his disciples came to him" (Matt. 5:1). Jesus did not shy away from preaching and teaching to large crowds as they came to him. This larger crowd included his closest followers (Matt. 4:18–22) and other people who were not yet committed followers of his who were eavesdropping on his teaching (Matt. 7:28–29).

However, Jesus did not just minister to large crowds. The crowds were often the recipients of Jesus' ministry (Matt. 9:36; 13:2), but there were also times when Jesus deliberately and intentionally moved away from the large crowds into smaller discipleship spaces (8:18; 13:36). He often created spaces and ministry environments that were only accessible to his closest followers. In these spaces he was more selective about what he was teaching. He was not changing the scope of his message—he continued to teach about the kingdom of God—but he was able to explain his message with greater depth. Even when he was ministering to the crowds, he intentionally found ways to give his closest followers greater access, more teaching, and even more of himself. For example, in Matthew 8:18 we see Jesus intentionally drawing closer to his immediate disciples by moving away from the larger crowd. Matthew tells us, "Now when Jesus saw a crowd around him, he gave orders to go over to the other side." He ordered his disciples to join him on his mission to a largely non-Jewish area, known as the Decapolis.[1] "And he called to him his twelve disciples and gave them authority over unclean spirits, to cast them out, and to heal every disease and every affliction" (Matt. 10:1). The rest

---

1. R. T. France, *The Gospel of Matthew,* New International Commentary on the New Testament (Grand Rapids, MI: Eerdmans, 2007), 325.

of chapter 10 includes specific teaching (scope) and intentional commissioning (sending) that the large crowds did not receive.

The point of scalability in Jesus's ministry is that he intentionally used various discipleship spaces to teach his disciples. He also had an intentional ministry scope, to teach his followers about the kingdom of God. He developed an intentional discipleship sequence that even continued in his resurrection and ascension, as he sent his Spirit to grow and equip his followers.

Finally, he did not settle with training his followers, but he sent all of his disciples to make more disciples. His message (scope) never changed: he came to proclaim the kingdom of God (Luke 4:43). But he did intentionally give more indepth teaching to his closest followers, and he eventually sent them out to proclaim the message of God's kingdom (Matt. 10:7). He also intentionally sequenced his discipleship. Some disciples were with Jesus for an afternoon, some were with him for weeks, and others were with him for years. Jesus intentionally invested in all the disciples, but he did not invest in them equally. In like manner, he did not send all disciples the same way, but instead he intentionally commissioned his followers in accordance with their training.

Can Your Church Implement This?

I completely understand how the busyness of ministry can be paralyzing. I also know how continually changing a philosophy of ministry can feel defeating. But I really believe that if you give intentional time—whether you're pastoring a large church or whether you find yourself in a much smaller ministry context, perhaps as a church planter or bivocational pastor—the strategy around deep discipleship can be implemented in virtually any local church context.

One of my friends from seminary works at a small Baptist church. His ministry context could not be more different from mine in terms of size of the church, ministry budget, and even cultural context. Over the last few years he and I have had several discussions about what it would look like for him to implement some of these ideas at his church. He was worried about whether this philosophy of ministry would work in his ministry context. There are only a few staff members and a little more than a hundred people. Now, three years after beginning to implement these concepts, they have a thriving and sustainable discipleship ministry.

The first thing they did was decide what discipleship spaces would be helpful in their context, and they settled on four discipleship spaces: classes, studies, a one-year discipleship program, and a residency program. Then they decided what their scope of discipleship would be. They decided that they wanted to train their church in Scripture, spiritual formation, and worldview/apologetics. Then they worked on how they would sequence these spaces in order to help facilitate depth and growth. Finally, they thought intentionally about where they would send the disciples they were training. Over the past three years they have implemented classes, most of which are taught by qualified laity. They have a men's and a women's Bible study of thirty to forty people each, which are taught by staff members, and the small group tables are facilitated by leaders in the congregation. They have started a one-year discipleship program that has eight to ten people in it each year, and they now have more than twenty graduates. They also started a residency program where they select two or three of the standouts from their one-year discipleship program and ask them to spend a year in a mentorship track.

Another pastor I know emailed me and asked if these ideas could be implemented in a small church plant just outside of Boston. For a few months we exchanged emails and had a few phone conversations, and I encouraged him to ask the questions we've been asking in this book. A few years later they have a thriving discipleship ministry, clarity around how they are trying to form and train their disciples, and have developed a missional mind-set in which all of their members feel called to the task of making more disciples.

If I have learned anything over the last several years in pastoral ministry, it is that this philosophy of ministry is scalable. Your church—regardless of its size, no matter what the budget is, and no matter what your facilities are—can do this.

How Can Your Church Implement This?

The final question we need to ask is the question of strategy: *How* can your church implement this? Of course, every church environment is a little bit different, which is why I have encouraged you to think about this through the lens of questions. I have not tried to give a prescription for how every church can do this, but rather I've allowed every church to answer these questions for themselves. However, I want to conclude with some principles about strategy that will help every church implement a philosophy of ministry that will, by God's grace, create a culture of deep discipleship. The following are principles I would encourage you to adhere to as you implement this philosophy of ministry: structure, predictability, accountability, accessibility, community, excellence (SPAACE).[2]

Structure

The first part of your strategy is to develop a structured approach to ministry. The trend over the past several years has been to develop approaches to local church ministry in more unstructured or organic ways. The question we generally ask is, "How do I help people develop healthy relationships in the

---

2. This is a strategy Jen Wilkin and I worked on together, and I am deeply indebted to her for helping me think through this. Additionally, this is the strategic framework we adopted at The Village Church in all of the discipleship ministries.

life of the local church?" This is an important question, and it reveals that the highest stated value of an unstructured organic approach to ministry is relationship. We are trying to free up calendars and commitments in order to free up time for people in their communities. Organic ministries operate from a high appreciation for relationships and for the priesthood of believers, things I appreciate as well.

But an organic or unstructured approach to ministry flows from the assumption that structure is inherently less capable of helping people develop deep relationships—an assumption I want to challenge. While I understand this approach has some benefits, I believe it has also come with a cost—a higher cost than we have realized. Unstructured approaches to ministry tend to be unreliable, they change regularly, and it can become difficult for participants to know what they are committing themselves to. This can actually be detrimental to relationships over time. A structured approach, on the other hand, is consistent and reliable, and offers a sort of relationship incubator. When people connect with other saints in a structured ministry context, it gives life to organic relationships that will grow and evolve for years to come—relationships that probably would never have been born without the original structured ministry context.

Rather than asking the question, "How do I help people develop healthy relationships in the life of the local church?," we should be asking the question, "How do we create structured environments and commitments for people in order to develop healthy relationships in the life of the church?" A structured approach to ministry is not rigid; it is reliable. Reliability is also a key ingredient in helping people build relationships. The challenge that more organic approaches to ministry can have is that the lack of structure over time will mean that people will be less committed. Your members are used to making commitments to things that are tangible, reliable, and structured.

For example, if you start a Whole 30 diet, join a CrossFit box, or start taking classes at a community college, you know exactly what you are committing to. In ministry, we often are not clear about what we are asking people to commit to, so they don't. If you are struggling to get people to commit, it is probably because you have not been clear about what you are asking them to commit to. We need to stop apologizing for asking people to commit to discipleship as if they are too busy. We often say things like, "We know how busy you are, and we are really sorry to ask this of you, but can you make space for this four-week Bible study on Ephesians?" We will never make deep disciples if we apologize when we ask people to make commitments—commitments that are often less significant than the other things in life they've already committed to doing.

People are not afraid of committing to things; they are afraid of committing to unreliable things. Our approach to ministry needs to be structured and reliable. People want to know what they are committing to. It is important, as you implement discipleship spaces, that you honor their commitment. The best and deepest spiritual formation happens when we clearly state the plan we are committed to, and we follow it. A structured approach to ministry will allow you to give people clear commitments to discipleship and, at the same time, will allow relationships to develop organically. But if you start by aiming at organic relationships, you'll never get people committed to discipleship spaces.

Predictability

The next part of your strategy is to develop ministry predictability. Similar to structure, people are used to living in a predictable rhythm of life—except for when it comes to the church. Your church should build its discipleship rhythms according to the rhythms of your people's lives, and it should stick to that pattern for a long time. Sometimes people are worried that a predictable ministry cycle reveals some lack of dependence upon the Spirit. They are concerned that predictability eventually leads to outdated ministry practices or dead religion. But the flip side is no less dangerous. Concern about a predictable approach to ministry leaves churches and organizations to constantly reinvent themselves, adapting new rhythms and new philosophies, and they find themselves on a constant treadmill of change. When we are changing our philosophy of ministry every few years, we lose credibility and trust with the people we are trying to shape and form.

On the other hand, when we develop predictable cycles, rhythms, and philosophies of ministry, we tend to gain trust with the people we are shaping and forming. Other institutions that want commitment from people understand this. School rhythms start and stop at the same time every year. Professional sports teams start and stop their season at the same time every year. Our entire world is based on predictable rhythms and commitments. Predictability is essential for building trust and credibility with your participants. As you are planning when to have events, or when to start and stop classes, you should consider the rhythm of your community, you should be aware of how your ministry rhythm may conflict with other commitments people have, and you should develop your structured approach to ministry around these predictable rhythms. Your ministry calendar should honor the schedules and follow the rhythms of your participants' lives.

For example, if you are going to have an eleven-week Bible study in the fall and the spring, the fall semester should start after Labor Day and end before Thanksgiving. The spring semester should start in late January, giving you enough time to end before Easter. Predictable rhythms are everywhere in our culture, and our participants depend on them in their everyday lives. When churches offer predictable rhythms, we will see the commitment levels of church members rise, and they will begin to see the church as a credible guide in their spiritual formation.

Predictable ministries adhere to the same pattern every year so your participants can anticipate and plan for when and where your meeting times occur.

Accountability

The next part of your strategy is to develop a culture of accountability. We've already discussed this briefly in a previous chapter, but I cannot emphasize its importance enough: one of the best things you can do for your people is to raise the bar for them. Too often we ask the question, "How can we lower the bar of entry?" But the better question is, "How can we raise the bar of discipleship?" Every one of your discipleship spaces—regardless of whether it is at the end of your sequence, like a residency, or one of the more accessible spaces, like a Bible study or class—must set clear expectations in terms of what you are expecting from each participant. Then hold them accountable to them.

I understand the impulse to lower the bar because we can think that more people will be involved if we lower the bar, but this has not been my experience. We often lower the bar so much that participation loses its value. We should lower obstacles to entry, but not expectations. People are eager to be called to something great, and the best way to do it is to set clear expectations and follow through on holding them accountable to meet those expectations.

A lot of the ways you can hold people accountable correspond to what an active learning environment looks like. For example, every discipleship space should have some standard for attendance. Every discipleship space should have some kind of prework—like reading or working on a curriculum. Prework tends to create dissonance for learners. They begin to realize what they do not know, so they start to ask questions and engage actively with the material. Dissonance is discipleship gold. You want your participants to feel the distance between where they are and where they want to be. They then come to the discipleship space, and before you teach them, they are given a second opportunity for accountability—a conversation with their small group before the teaching time. Learning happens in community, and they will feel a sense of accountability when they know they are going to have a conversation about the material before they are taught. Third, they are accountable to come to the teaching session, which should help relieve some of the dissonance they felt in the prework. Finally, there should be an expectation that they are having conversations about the material and teaching others.

Prework, group discussion, group teaching, articulation to others—this is how learning and growth happen in real life. We have forgotten that in the church. Accountability is important for your discipleship strategy. Discipleship accountability means you are going to hold your participants accountable to prepare, attend, and contribute to the discipleship space. They are not going to simply come and learn from you, but you are going to hold them accountable to contributing to an active learning environment.

Accessibility

The next part of your ministry strategy is accessibility. By accessibility, we are talking about two things: teaching in an accessible way and making the learning spaces accessible to people by removing obstacles.

First, you need to make sure you are teaching in accessible ways, depending on the discipleship space and sequence. Instruction and participation are given at the appropriate level of the learning space. In a residency style or mentorship program, you should be teaching at a higher accessibility level than a class and vice versa. Put simply, discipleship ministry should be done at a level that is appropriate to that space by considering what resources, terminology, prework, and teaching will encourage participants to take the next step in their discipleship journey. If you teach at too high a level, you run the risk of intimidating your participants. If you teach at too low a level, you run the risk of patronizing and boring your participants. Good teachers know where their participants are and they meet them there, but they do not let them stay there.

Most of your participants think biblical, theological, and spiritual development are only for the elite. Creating accessible learning environments and discipleship spaces shows them that theology is for everybody. The Bible is meant to be read by every single person. Spiritual formation is for every single disciple of Jesus. One of the ways pastors and churches can make learning environments accessible is by becoming theological translators. For example, if you wanted to teach on the incarnation, they might be intimidated to read St. Athanasius's *On the Incarnation*. Once they have read the book and you meet with them and show them how this work translates to their everyday life, they will learn that theology is actually accessible to them.

Second, your church should think through ways it can partner with your members to remove obstacles to their participation in your discipleship spaces. This was a huge area of growth and development for our church. We had unintentionally placed the burden of discipleship on individual people. We were insistent, and rightly so, that we did not want to foster a culture of consumerism, but we swung the pendulum too far and actually made it hard for people to get involved. For example, we had to learn how to think intentionally about the obstacles a single mom might have in getting involved in our various discipleship spaces. When we thought through this lens, offering childcare became a no-brainer.

Accessibility also means thinking intentionally about what time you are offering discipleship opportunities. If you're offering a women's Bible study during the day, you are going to have a lot of stay-at-home moms participate, which is incredible. But you might miss a lot of working women, which means you should probably have an additional Bible study at night. Does your community with men who travel during the week for their job get filled? If so, you should think about placing your men's Bible study on the weekend. Again, all of our contexts are going to be slightly different, but deep discipleship-oriented churches are working hard at thinking clearly and carefully about making our discipleship spaces as accessible to as many participants as possible.

Community

The next part of your ministry strategy is to make sure everything is built around community. There is no such thing as lone-ranger discipleship, so all of your discipleship spaces should center around community. When you build a philosophy of ministry around structure and predictability, community will naturally happen. I have tried to show how important community is to the discipleship process. Community is not discipleship, but discipleship cannot happen without community. Your strategy should look for ways to help your participants form deep relationships with one another. Their main relationship should not be with you but with other participants and colearners.

One way to foster deep community in your learning environments is to make sure people are not seated in rows but in circles. In every single learning space we have worked hard at making sure we had round tables where people could discuss, learn from one another, and articulate questions to one another. This has fostered some of the most beautiful Christian community I have ever seen. It is beautiful when people begin to realize that they are responsible not just for their individual discipleship but for the building up of the whole body.

Excellence

The final part of your ministry strategy is to consistently pursue excellence. The church, of all places, should be the place where we do what we say we are going to do. One of the worst things we can do is call people to high standards of excellence while failing to meet them ourselves. It is important that you work hard and do your best for the glory of God. I think sometimes we are scared to call one another to excellence in ministry because we are somehow afraid that excellence is opposed to grace. It's important for pastors and churches to recognize that excellence is not antithetical to grace; grace fuels our drive for excellence. Our discipleship ministries should all strive toward excellence, primarily because we are trying to reflect the excellencies of God.

Deep discipleship will flourish in the local church when we align ourselves with this strategy:

1. STRUCTURE: Offer structured discipleship spaces that honor the participants' commitment.
2. PREDICTABILITY: Operate with predictable rhythms, not changing our discipleship offerings too frequently.
3. ACCCOUNTABILITY: Hold people accountable in ways that are consistent with the discipleship space.
4. ACCESSIBILITY: Make our discipleship spaces accessible to participants through accessible content and by removing obstacles for people.
5. COMMUNITY: Center all learning and discipleship around community.
6. EXCELLENCE: Pursue excellence in the local church for the glory of Christ.

Deep Discipleship in the Local Church

So, what does it look like to be a church that finds its purpose in a culture of deep discipleship that is making holistic disciples of Jesus? What does the win look like? It looks like local churches being reminded that they are the primary place

God creates holistic followers of Christ. Local churches will retrieve learning spaces and apprenticeship as necessary environments. We will know what the scope of discipleship is, what disciples need. We will know how to grow disciples, not just keep disciples. And the local church will train everyone we send and send everyone we train.

Deep discipleship is all about helping people find greater and deeper enjoyment in the Triune God. My greatest hope, now at the conclusion of the book, is that our ministries, churches, sermons, curriculum, community groups—everything we are giving ourselves to in ministry—would help people come to see God for who he is, an inexhaustible depth of never-ending perfection. My hope is that the local church would be the primary place where we introduce people to all that is in God. My hope is that our churches would begin, and continue, to reflect the deep excellencies that can only be found in the Triune God. We can pursue deep discipleship with him because his beauty and excellency know no depth. Everything else we pursue in this life will come to an end; only deep discipleship will continue into eternal life.

Main Ideas

1. Instead of asking, "Can my church do this?," ask the better question, "Why would my church *not* do this?"

2. Deep discipleship does not require massive resources, a large congregation, or an enormous ministry staff.

3. We will never make deep disciples if we apologize when we ask people to make commitments.

Questions for Discussion

1. Discuss the ministry strategy of Jesus. Is it fair to say he operated with a sort of scope and sequence of deep discipleship?

2. Discuss the following principles used in the acronym SPAACE (structure, predictability, accountability, accessibility, community, excellence). Do you agree with each of these values? Is there anything you would add? Which of these would be the most difficult for your church to commit to?

3. At the end of this book, are you in any way still unconvinced of the need for deep discipleship in the local church? Is there any reason you think your church can't do this?

To-Do List

1. Apply the SPAACE acronym to your working scope and sequence of discipleship. What would it look like to operate each ministry or program in your scope and sequence with each of these values?

2. You should now have something close to a complete plan for deep discipleship in your church. Now talk about a plan for rolling it out. What does your timeline look like? Whom do you need to get on board as early adopters? Who in your church will champion the cause of deep discipleship?

3. Close your time by praying together again, asking God for guidance and wisdom, asking him to glorify himself by making the knowledge of him cover your church like the waters cover the sea.

Epilogue

I want to end the book by going back to the beginning. I believe the church has misdiagnosed our discipleship disease. We all know we have a disease, but most of us are mistreating the disease. We have developed ministry paradigms that ask less of people, not more of people. We have adopted strategies that appeal to the lowest common denominator and let them stay there. We have asked our pastors to be marketers. We are trying to simply keep the crowd instead of trying to grow Christians. We have settled for a shallow version of discipleship, while Christ invites all of us deeper.

The reason we go deeper is because God is who he says he is. He is an inexhaustible well of perfections. He is everlasting glory. He is never-ending in his righteousness. He is bottomless in his beauty. Deep discipleship matters not because it is a philosophy of ministry, but because of who God is. Deep discipleship matters because we should all want more of God. Deep discipleship is ultimately an invitation into a God-centered vision of all things. If we have a great philosophy of ministry that does not lead us to the great God, then we are wasting our time. Deep discipleship is all about pointing our people, our resources, and our churches toward Christ and his kingdom.

While I was writing this book I transitioned from being a pastor at The Village Church in Flower Mound, Texas, where I oversaw The Village Church Institute, to being the lead pastor of Storyline Fellowship in Arvada, Colorado. Being a pastor at The Village was one of the greatest privileges of my ministry career. The men and women of that church love God, love the Bible, are full of the Holy Spirit, and they live on mission. We founded the Institute in order to see people go deeper in their relationship with God, and we were blown away by what we saw. The people of TVC did not want less Bible; they wanted more Bible. They did not want less theology; they wanted more theology. They did not want less spiritual discipline; they wanted more spiritual discipline. The convictions in this book are what led me to start and found The Village Church Institute, and God answered our prayers far more than we ever could have expected.

At the same time, it is the convictions in this book that led me to this new ministry post as a lead pastor. I want to ask these same questions in a new context, in a new city, in a new culture, and among a new people. My hope is that not only the people of Storyline Fellowship, but also the people in your ministry context will love God more because you read this book.

Whether you serve as a discipleship pastor, a lead pastor, a groups pastor, a women's ministry leader, or you are simply a Christian who wants to grow in their love and knowledge of God, my hope for you is that the convictions outlined in this book would take root in your own ministry context. That you would ask better questions—questions that will lead to a better philosophy of ministry. Questions that hopefully will not just lead to a better philosophy of ministry, but to transformed lives that are growing deeper into fellowship with the Triune God.